T0150447

PORTFOLIO
THE RIGHT CHOICE

Shiv Shivakumar, or Shiv as he is popularly known, is one of India's longest-serving CEOs. He is currently the group executive president at Aditya Birla Group. He has worked across multiple industries and categories, and has handled over sixty brands in his career. He was CEO for Nokia in India and subsequently led the company's emerging markets unit; he was also chairman and CEO for PepsiCo South Asia. He is regarded as one of India's leading management and leadership thinkers and speakers.

THE RIGHT CHOICE

RESOLVING 10 CAREER DILEMMAS FOR EXTRAORDINARY SUCCESS

SHIV SHIVAKUMAR

PORTFOLIO
PENGUIN

An imprint of Penguin Random House

PORTFOLIO

USA | Canada | UK | Ireland | Australia
New Zealand | India | South Africa | China

Portfolio is part of the Penguin Random House group of companies
whose addresses can be found at global.penguinrandomhouse.com

Published by Penguin Random House India Pvt. Ltd
7th Floor, Infinity Tower C, DLF Cyber City,
Gurgaon 122 002, Haryana, India

Penguin
Random House
India

First published in Portfolio by Penguin Random House India 2021

ISBN 9780670095698

Typeset in Adobe Garamond Pro by Manipal Technologies Limited, Manipal
Printed at Thomson Press India Ltd, New Delhi

www.penguin.co.in

Heartfelt thanks to my mother, Ms Seeta,
my siblings, Viji and Raman,
and my wife, Hamsini

Contents

Foreword

Every career is a series of opportunities and challenges. There is no set formula to manage a career as the world and the context of any business evolves continuously. Some navigate the journey well because they are self-aware to recognize an opportunity or face up to a challenge. Many struggle.

I am really glad Shiv is writing about this difficult subject of career dilemmas—the many crossroads we face. I remember our conversation over coffee some eighteen months ago. It is wonderful to see him bring this topic to life in an informative and engaging way.

The ten career dilemmas Shiv talks about cover an entire career spanning from management trainee to managing director. If you do not have a personal coach or mentor, you can turn to this book as your guide. Eleven CEOs, six entrepreneurs and six HR practitioners have all shared their wisdom for your benefit. I am particularly happy that the list includes eleven women leaders, bringing in much richness to the various perspectives.

I wish I had had the benefit of this book early in my life. Shiv is uniquely qualified to compile this book. He has worked his way up from the position of a management trainee to that of an MD. He is an observer of people, a great leader with a lot of heart; he is a voracious reader, a wonderful listener. I saw it all upfront, in person.

Enjoy the book. Take charge of your career, resolve your dilemmas and choose wisely the best path forward.

New York   Indra Nooyi
December 2020

Introduction

The idea behind this book took root about eighteen months ago. My original thoughts revolved around temptations that arise in a career and how to deal with them. When discussing the idea with Indra Nooyi at her home in Chennai, we both felt that 'temptations' sounded sinful and worthy of rejection, whereas, with 'dilemma', I would actually be talking about the very real scenario many experience—of being faced with two attractive alternatives. And that's how *10 Career Dilemmas* was born.

A year ago, I bumped into Ram Charan, my guru for two decades. He would always encourage me to write a book. He listened keenly as I fleshed out my ideas for *10 Career Dilemmas*, and giving me an instant thumbs up, he remarked, 'Interesting topic, no one has addressed it!'

So here I am, with a book that explores the myriad career dilemmas people come across and how careers take shape.

A career is lived forward but understood backwards, once you are nearly done with it.

Careers rarely follow a straight-line path or a neat upward curve unlike what most business articles, leadership interviews and speeches would have us believe. The most successful careers are, in fact, a set of zigzag patterns, marked by spells of stagnation, interspersed with rapid growth.

What constitutes a good career?

A good career is one where you learn at the start, then go on to contribute at the end when you multiply that learning, coupled with all the experience and wisdom garnered along the way. Most people have a fund of youthful energy early on in their careers, while older people have the gift of wisdom gained from experience and a few knocks sustained over the course of the journey. The right balance comes at the age of around forty-two, when a manager typically has an optimal proportion of energy and wisdom. Becoming the best in your field and being acknowledged as such is a good marker of a successful career for many. Becoming the CEO of a small or large company is another marker. All said and done, a career should not culminate on a note of disgrace nor should it end in a whimper, that is, go unnoticed. Making a difference is an important aspect of a career well lived.

Nevertheless, what defines a good career is in itself a dilemma!

A career is one of the most important things every manager spends a lot of time actively thinking about, pouring ample energy into shaping and moulding it, dreaming big about it and living it.

I am privileged and lucky to have had a good career, spanning many industries and varied assignments. I started out in oral care, did stints in beverages, personal products, food and beverage, and am currently involved with the building construction industry and the global textiles market. I have worked with Hindustan Unilever, Nokia, PepsiCo and ABG, to name a few—a graph I could never have known I would script when I first began. And that is not to say I am a rolling stone either; I've had long and fulfilling stints in all the companies I worked in.

When I pause and look back at the road travelled, all I can say is that it happened, for I never willed it in any particular direction. At the start of my career, I only wanted to be a good marketing guy, whatever that meant. Back in college, I remember reading every article and book I could lay my hands on, on marketing and strategy. I ended up spending half my career as a CEO, something I never imagined even in my wildest dreams!

In this wide-ranging journey, I have seen the good, the bad and the ugly of organizations, processes and people. I have, first and foremost, been a company man. I have had the chance to work with some great colleagues and wonderful peers, and I have learnt from each and every one of them. At least fifty to seventy of my colleagues/subordinates are in CEO and CXO roles. A fact that gives me immense pride, knowing that the path I charted is, in a way, my own little contribution.

I have seen careers flourish and careers flounder. When I look closely at the ones that floundered, I realize that they made the wrong choice when faced with a dilemma. And in all likelihood, what made matters worse was that they probably did not have access to good advice; if they had, it could have helped them make better decisions, smarter and wiser choices.

Which is why I believe this book will have relevance and resonate with you, my readers.

From the plethora of both successful and unsuccessful careers I have seen and studied over decades, I summarize here my five big career lessons:

Lesson 1: There is no Manual 101 for a successful career.

If there were, so many people would have cracked it by now. A career is not a college examination where you can prepare beforehand and go max on a subject.

Nothing can truly prepare you for a career. The best prepared, the most intelligent, the shrewdest and the most politically sharp types have all bitten the dust at some point or other, and people wonder what went wrong. Having a good career requires many things to work in tandem—your talent, your readiness, the right roles opening at the right time, the right role that helps you create impact, how key people in the industry and the ecosystem regard you, and of course, finally, a bit of luck.

Careers in business are similar to those in show business. Context and timing are all too important for a movie to be successful and for a movie star to be noticed. Sheer craft alone does not ensure success.

Lesson 2: No two careers are alike, even though candidates may well have many things in common.

You cannot blindly copy someone else's career path and wish for similar results. There is no Xerox copy machine at work here! India boasts of housing the maximum number of business schools in the world, a majority chunk out of a global count of 12,000. We produce close to half a million MBAs every year. If you were to examine bare statistics, less than 5 per cent of an IIM batch makes it to the CEO's office. So, merely possessing a degree from a prestigious institute doesn't guarantee anything. An MBA is a degree, not a passport to greener pastures. The MBA degree, at best, opens the first door to a company and a window to the second company. Beyond that, it's your own perseverance and performance that matter.

A career is built on the foundation of working well with people. No B-school can teach you the nuances of people dynamics involved, because all of it is contextual. People can both make you and break you. I have been part of smart teams that delivered nothing and I have been part of teams of committed people who delivered well beyond their potential. Holding every successful team together is a chemistry that can never be found in any textbook nor can it be manufactured by policy; it just happens, and good leaders understand that. Down to the wire, it is the trust that people have or do not have in your values. Trust, simply put, boils down to this maxim: You will not take advantage of me nor hurt me when I am vulnerable.

Lesson 3: Timing is of paramount importance for a good career.

Ask any CEO, and they will tell you that they were ready for the job a few years *before* they got the job. If you are good, many people will give you strong roles. From the time I became general manager, I have had a fair share of excellent roles offered to me many times through my career. But each time, for one reason or the other, I didn't make the move, either due to the circumstances of the company I was in or a promise I had made to stay for a certain period. I got some outstanding roles when Nokia was flourishing, and then again when it was floundering, but when Nokia was floundering was precisely the wrong time I felt to move on. So, loyalty and the context made me stay. One tough truth I have learnt about timing is that the emotional state you are in has a vital role to play. If you are unhappy in your current company, then any role that comes your way looks very good. The best career moves are those that are made when you are happy in your current company and then a better role comes along to take you out of your current company. That's a rational decision.

It is unlikely that we will see people spend all their time in one company; that would be rare and, in many cases, not valued by anyone in a rapidly changing world. I have worked in four large organizations, all very different, and, every time, I learnt both from the company and the industry.

Lesson 4: A good career reaches out beyond your job's boundaries in making a contribution.

It is not just about doing well in the company you work in; rather, it is just as important to be part of the industry body, to contribute in related fields, such as academia. Focusing on the job alone will not take you to your destination. People in the ecosystem should see you as a thought leader, someone with the versatility to do different things. Giving to society is important from a career standpoint. You build the career path of your choice when you knock on the doors of senior management; it is not the company, certainly not your boss, and least of all the HR manager who determine your course.

A worthwhile career holds good for about thirty-plus years in today's world. The average life span of a company is under twenty years, so in many cases, good careers outlive companies. In the future, I think people would opt for a combination of paid and unpaid work to nurture what gives them satisfaction or meaning.

Another element that you may encounter is the media, and you must learn how to deal with it prudently. The media is neither a friend nor an adversary, but you should recognize that it does have a role to play when it comes to your readers and those who learn from you. I must admit that, by and large, the media has been rather fair to me throughout my career. I owe them a lot for their support.

Lesson 5: The maturity to deal with frustrations at work.

If you are capable, it is likely that you will attract some amount of envy or dislike, especially from your peer group, and in some cases, from incompetent and insecure superiors as well. This would pose a challenge and create tension for you, since you want to do well for the company.

You must have the maturity to deal with this. In one of the companies I worked for, I would find that a person entering a new role would first spend a year dissing his predecessor, and then do whatever he needed to afterwards. I found this to be a colossal waste of time. I have never ever run down my predecessor in any role that I have taken on. From the day I stepped into the role, I have given it my best shot and only tried to improve the situation from where it stood earlier. Indra Nooyi actually commented on this point when she wrote to my mother in 2015. It was kind of her to notice and give credit for the fact that I never rubbished past managers.

While you get credit for your predecessor's actions, you need to be smart about handling the downside without being a spoilt child about it.

Coming to the other side of the equation, I have always endeavoured to give my successors the best handover possible. I gave the best handover to Vinod Nambiar as sales manager in Hindustan Unilever, to Mukul Deoras as category head in Hindustan Unilever, and to Arto Numella as CEO, emerging markets in Nokia. I still have the documents I made for them. It is important to create a valuable legacy when you execute a great handover.

All careers are built on good health, strong emotional anchors in the form of people who support you through the ups and downs in your career, and your ability to learn and stay relevant all the time. Today, a career is a very public-persona entity, what with the range of print and audio-visual media, social media, glass door ratings, etc., that go with the territory. You have to build your reputation and safeguard it in order to steer it in the right direction.

This book is all about the different dilemmas you face in a career where many alternatives may look good but you still have to make a choice. It aims to equip you to smoothly navigate your career journey—a dream journey everyone sets out on wanting to progress from management trainee to the coveted position of managing director. Very few actually get there, but there is no ban or tax on dreaming it, and more importantly, no harm in every individual working towards that goal. Ultimately, this book is for those who are only just starting off, for those looking for growth in middle management, and for everyone who wishes to have a dream career.

I have outlined the ten most common dilemmas and have got people who surmounted them to talk about their experiences. I have also documented the viewpoints of some of India's best people managers on these dilemmas.

We face a constant barrage of dilemmas as we chart our careers. Every year, we ask ourselves whether our efforts have been rewarded, whether we are progressing fast enough, whether we are worthy of a promotion. And every year, we want to do more, achieve more, be recognized more. Our innate self-worth, effort and ambition combine to make us question alternatives presented to us. These alternatives are all dilemmas to be resolved.

For example, I have seen an unhappy brand manager in an FMCG company choose money and switch over to a bank, solely for the monetary jump. I have seen an established professional leave his company to join a smaller company because he wanted to be a vice president by the age of forty. I have seen a consultant opt for the CEO role in a small company in a dying industry only because he wanted his CV to carry the tag of a young CEO. I have also seen people stick with a company through thick and thin and patiently wait for their chance to move ahead. In a vast majority of cases, sadly, the wife sacrifices a lot for her husband's career. But things are changing now. I know of men who sacrifice their career for their spouse. A very good colleague of mine chose to be based out of Chennai to be able to look after his parents, instead of moving to senior roles available in Mumbai. There are couples who live apart, in different cities or even countries, to ensure smooth continuity of school education for their children. Each of these individuals were up against a dilemma and resorted to their own methods to make a choice.

The dilemmas I share here aren't sourced from any textbook. Textbooks tend to be prescriptive; they are meant for the masses, they don't specify the individual dimension. They present a few models and the two-by-two matrix—the staple breakfast of all MBAs! While textbooks are logical, real life isn't—it is a rich combination of logic and magic. Sometimes magic wins, other times logic does.

The ten dilemmas presented in this book are drawn from my varied observations and experiences over the years. They contain an even blend of logic and magic in them, where the best people talk of the magic of how they resolved the dilemma. All of these were actual situations faced by people in some manner, shape or form, at some point in their professional journey.

My objective behind sharing these learnings is to help readers form a better understanding and appreciation of such scenarios. They could benefit from the mistakes and wisdom of others who have been in similar situations, which could make them better prepared to deal with these and other, similar dilemmas. Ultimately, that would hopefully facilitate a greater sense of resilience and maturity to manage such conflicted alternatives better.

A career is much like a marathon; you need to pace yourself. There are bound to be twists and turns, and your determination and persistence are what will get you to the finish line. The finish line, of course, is what you define it to be. For many people, it is becoming a CEO or the head of an institution in their field, be it as a dean or a director, a college principal or an army general.

While writing this book, I reached out to a few people whom I would term the inner board. I described my book and mission to them. All of them had similar inputs to offer. They advised that I must stay true to the soul of who I was and reflect the same in my writing. So I thought about it, and I believe the very soul of who I have been as a writer and speech maker all these years is embodied in these three fundamental things:

a. Positive, authentic, inspiring messages
b. Data turned into insights
c. Memorable anecdotes gleaned from every experience

Dear readers, it is my fond hope that this book will help you better navigate the many twists and turns you encounter as you head towards conquering the milestones and successfully reaching the finish line you have set yourself in your career.

Do enjoy the read, and I wish you the very best ahead.

Dilemma 1

Is Money the Most Important Variable in a Career?

I once said in an IIM convocation address I delivered: 'Don't measure yourself by the money you make. If you are good, money will follow you. However, if you have money, it doesn't mean you are good. Try and be very good.'

I must add that while money cannot buy us happiness, it certainly is a safeguard against sorrow.

A successful career is not about money alone; it cannot be as unidimensional as that. Our goals extend beyond just making a certain amount of money, even though we may never consciously realize it. We work for affiliation to an institution, recognition in the company and industry fora, acknowledgement and appreciation from peers, as also stability and peace of mind.

However, we get swayed by external factors such as media reportage and industry comparisons in terms of salaries and earnings, and tend to use these as superfluous benchmarks of our worth and standing. This pattern sets in at the engineering college or business school itself.

Come placement season, every business school reports the top-salaried job and the average salary offered on campus. There is a race amongst business schools, with each vying to be seen as better than the rest solely on the basis of this parameter; students crave to gain admission into such an institute. As with any data point, the data quoted by a number of schools is misleading but it becomes a yardstick. Since all business schools do not make their calculations in the same way, there is scope for interpretation.

Similarly, every newspaper and magazine maintains a list of the highest-paid executives. But these lists simply do not capture what these top executives do beyond the figures they make, which makes the public question their worth. I recall an instance when the CEO of a BFSI (Banking, Financial Services and Insurance) company figured in one such list and a lot of investors, company employees and industry experts seriously questioned the value and contribution of that individual.

Without a doubt, money is a significant variable in every career. In many cases, people choose the job that offers them a higher salary; it is indeed as straightforward as that. In the Indian context, salary and benefits feature right on top in the list of criteria evaluated when choosing a company.

This focus on money does not surprise me; we do live in an uncertain world. No one is sure of company survival, or even industry survival, so people commit to the job and company at best for two to three years. Naturally, in that short timeframe, they would like to consolidate their gains. And the one thing they can affix a tangible value to is the monetary aspect. They cannot possibly put a tangible cap on skills or learning or culture. Hence, it boils down to maximizing money, which means maximizing the short term! Money is also a solid variable to boast about among friends and family, because we associate it with prestige and security.

I would like you to think about this variable called money differently.

Now, I know that many aspirants avail of student loans to pursue an MBA. Repaying that loan is top priority in their mind and so, on completing the academic course, they look for the highest-paying job offer.

A young, newly minted manager wants to buy the latest gadgets and fancy bikes, eat at the fanciest restaurants and hang out in the coolest places, buy a swanky car and go on luxurious holidays. During this phase, most people save little.

When they move into middle management, people worry about building a roof over their head. At this stage, many take loans to build assets based on the assumption that they have at least twenty years of a career ahead of them. Sometimes, this assumption turns out right, but in today's times this is not a guaranteed, valid assumption anymore. Over the last two decades, I have seen this premise hold true for fewer and fewer people.

Once they become senior managers, people seek to provide for their children's education, caregiving for aged parents, spending liberally on significant social events, such as religious ceremonies and weddings and so on.

A look at the annual earnings potential minus the annual spending reveals that people have a surplus in their bank account when in senior managerial positions. So, it is surprising when young people quit and move jobs for just a little more money, because that is immaterial in the long run. My advice to young managers, that is, to anyone below the age of thirty, is to maximize their learning and work at a place where they can multiply their capabilities rather than choosing money as the variable to maximize. This choice will not hurt them.

One question I am often asked is whether money matters to millennials as much as it did to previous generations. Millennials, as Deloitte puts it, are not that different on the issue of money; they differ on the savings aspect. 'More than half want to earn high salaries and be wealthy. But their priorities have evolved, or at least been delayed by financial or other constraints. Having children, buying homes, and other traditional signals of adult success markers do not top their list of ambitions,' says Deloitte's global millennial report of 2019. Instead, it points out, the focus is on travel, community, work-life balance and experiences. The average Indian saves about 20 per cent of his/her salary, while the millennial saves about 11 per cent. The latter tends to splurge more on experiences, and of course, compared with the earlier generation, the millennial is spoilt for choice.

So, if millennials are, more or less, the same when it comes to money, how are they different from previous generations at the workplace? Millennials value the total experience at work. They want the company to be tech-savvy, have the latest tech gadgets or platforms or software to work with. They want their work to be noticed, but they want to be rewarded for their talent and not just noticed for their success or failure. And they want that recognition immediately. As evidence, see the number of millennials posting their awards and recognitions on LinkedIn. They value breaks. They quote examples from Finland and New Zealand to make their case. They want to give unvarnished feedback to their staid bosses. They want less seriousness, less fuddy-duddyness at work. They don't think much of 'dog work'. I personally believe that they will change and veer closer to mainstream ideology in a few years' time, after taking a few knocks on the ideology they currently espouse. I remember Vipul Prakash and Gaurav running an advertisement for 7UP (the popular soft drink) at PepsiCo. The advertisement was aimed at millennials with society asking them whether they would marry the girl they were dating, about what they wanted to do in the future, whether they would stick with their job and so on. The answer to all those questions was 'I don't know'. Traditionally, parents and bosses expect you to know and cannot deal with this uncertainty-ridden 'I don't know' response.

India is home to the highest population of millennials in the world, but also accounts for nearly half of its working-age population. We will be the millennial capital of the world by 2040.

Are we converging with global variables when it comes to choice of employer? Randstad's latest survey pegs work-life balance (46 per cent) almost at par with salary expectations (47 per cent) in the Indian job seekers' criteria, just like their overseas peers. The job security plank held firmly by the baby boomers (those born around the 1960s) has been pushed to third place (41 per cent). This was pre-COVID, and I think we will see a change in the coming year.

TOP CRITERIA FOR INDIANS CHOOSING AN EMPLOYER

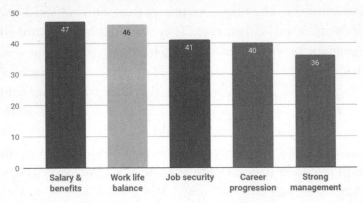

Source: Randstad Employer Brand Research Survey, 2019

The EVP (Employee Value Proposition) is obviously different for millennials versus senior managers. The higher up an executive, the more the importance given to salary and benefits as an EVP. Please note that the generation following the millennials—Gen Z—ascribes an even higher value to salary and benefits as compared to the millennials!

EVP DRIVER IMPORTANCE BY AGE (SALARY & BENEFITS)

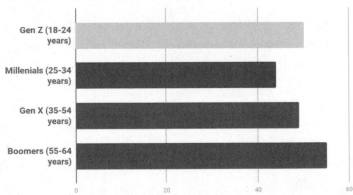

Source: Randstad Employer Brand Research Survey, 2019

This is understandable as people above fifty are at a different stage of life, handling responsibilities around children's education and marriage, aged parents' healthcare, and perhaps securing a home of their own.

Do Millennials and Other Generations Stay in a Company if Paid Well?

This question throws up a funny dichotomy. Money is the top reason to pick a company, but it is not the top reason to leave a company.

Let's start with tenure. Half the millennials in the world plan to quit their jobs in a year's time; this is up from 36 per cent in 2017. The corresponding number in India would be similar. That's why the millennials are called the 'job hopping' generation.

The primary reasons for quitting are: dissatisfaction with career path (43 per cent), work-life balance (36 per cent) and low compensation (33 per cent). No doubt, they leave a job

WHY INDIANS LEAVE THEIR JOBS

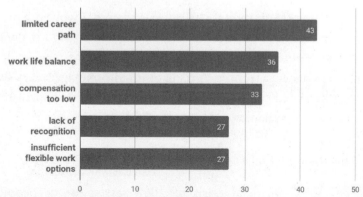

Source: Randstad Employer Brand Research Survey, 2019

for these reasons but money again is the basis on which they accept the next job offer!

Let's look at why people stay with a company. I think this will undergo a sea change after COVID. From 2019 data, we see that job security (45 per cent) is the most important parameter, with work-life balance and salary and benefits (40 per cent) coming in second.

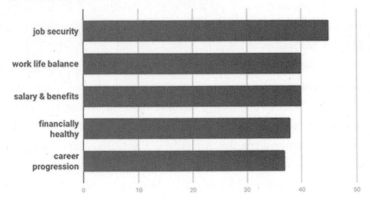

Source: Randstad Employer Brand Research Survey, 2019

There are organizational challenges and costs involved when people move jobs. When attrition is high, execution is poor and costs of recruitment, training and settling down go up. In my experience, a frontline person or middle manager takes six months to come up to speed, and those six months constitute a cost few companies compute.

The Role of Debt

The global financial crisis of 2008 saw a lot of people switching jobs in India. I got a consulting firm to look at the data and give us insights into the trend. We came to a clear correlation. Any executive who had an EMI (Equated Monthly Instalment payment) of more than 25 per cent of the take-home salary was constantly in the job market. The objective of the job hunt was to bring that EMI down to 10 per cent of take-home salary; at 25 per cent, they were worried. I think this is valid even today.

In the COVID phase, what people have not had control over is repayments. Repayments as a percentage of monthly household expenditure has dropped by 200 basis points in the second half of 2020.

The financial situation is tough and, therefore, money again becomes the variable to live for.

Worldwide, more than half the millennials believe their personal financial situation will worsen or stay the same. The situation is no better in India. Salary growth dipped to single digits in 2018, as per Aon Hewitt, even though it was the highest inflation-adjusted salary increase across APAC countries. In the past, a 12 to 15 per cent salary hike seemed like a birthright!

India Annual Salary Increase Between 2010 - 2018 (P)

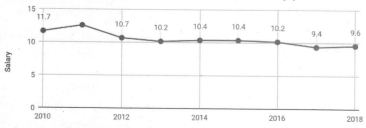

Source: Aon Hewitt Salary Increase Survey

Millennials Do Spend

Millennials are spearheading growth in credit; they are less afraid of taking on more debt for travel and other expenses. In India, household debt has more than doubled since the start of the decade, going from $120 billion in 2008 to around $300 billion in 2018. While debt boosts consumption and GDP growth in the short run (one-year period), it has a negative impact on growth in the long run. India's household debt-to-GDP ratio is still quite low (around 11 per cent) compared to other BRICS nations, but it can become a cause for worry if India gravitates towards being an EMI nation.

India household debt

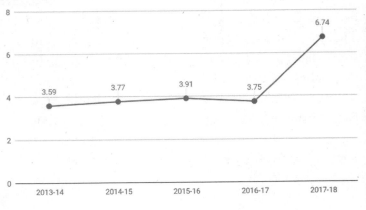

Source: RBI

In the cult Hindi film *Deewaar*, the mother (played by Nirupa Roy) asks the upright police officer son (played by Shashi Kapoor) why the well-to-do smuggler son (played by Amitabh Bachchan) isn't sleeping well. Shashi Kapoor's reply aptly sums up the dilemma: 'Money is a funny thing, Mom. You have too much of it and you can't sleep; you have too little of it and you still can't sleep.'

Harish Devarajan, leadership coach

Harish Devarajan is a leadership coach, consultant and independent director. A commerce graduate from XLRI (1985) specializing in human resources (HR), his first job was with Sundaram Fasteners, following which he joined Hindustan Lever Limited. After several years of working across functions, but primarily in HR at Hindustan Unilever Ltd, he rose to be head of HR there. In his mid-forties he quit the corporate rat race and founded People Unlimited, where he supports corporate leaders in their pursuit of excellence in organization performance and leadership effectiveness. He serves on the board of Bank of India as an independent director.

How important do you think money is in the context of jobs today? Is it still the primary driver?

I think that money as an element will continue to be important. At one point of time, it is probably a hygiene factor; at another point of time, it is a pride factor. Money may never be called out as the *most important* factor, but it is one of the important ones. It is not politically correct to say I am joining this company for money or I am leaving this company for money, and therefore people will never call it out. But it will always be one of the deciding factors. Some companies say they will not pay you much but will give you other opportunities, exposure, etc. All of that is good, but it does not substitute money.

How can one provide job security to employees today?

I don't think any company can commit to job security today. The business itself is not secure. It's more about how companies can provide a sense of stability to the individual. Quite a number of organizations have processes and systems in place saying that anybody can apply for any job, but they are not released because their immediate boss needs them in that particular position. These are things that make longevity for an individual difficult.

How does an employee judge the culture of a company and what should HR do to ensure that culture is consistent?

This is a topic I am interested in. There are two different kinds of cultures. There is a culture or value which is core and another culture or value which is transactional. So, when people talk about culture, sometimes they talk about the core culture which is really intrinsic and which is a signal element of that organization.

The Tatas, as an organization, symbolize integrity and trust. That is their core culture. On the other hand, we have the culture of action orientation. That is not necessarily an intrinsic culture; it is more a culture brought about by leaders at that point in time. And this transactional or transient culture may appear as an island within an organization. So, if you have a hundred leaders, some of them are action-oriented while some others may be very considered and plan-oriented instead. Now that is not the culture of the organization.

HR needs to be clear in terms of what they are touting as the culture of the organization. So while those intrinsic things are important, leadership styles are often mistaken to be culture. The intrinsic culture needs to be imbibed by people across the organization, by leaders, departments and units across the organization, for which a lot of communication, preparation and support is required.

Now, how do people judge cultures? Employees are able to judge cultures based on what they experience— not once, not twice, but on a continuous basis. Not in any one or two places, but across the organization. That will be possible only if there is a plan and an efficient way of making sure that people are aware of the culture, that leaders actually live the culture and develop their successors in such a way as to follow the same culture. For this to happen, HR needs to look carefully at the appointment of leaders, their development, and at holding them accountable for continuance and upkeep of the culture.

R.R. Nair, leadership coach and independent director, Ex-HR, Unilever

R.R. Nair is a much sought-after coach. He is coach to several CXOs and CEOs across large Indian and multinational organizations and consults on HR strategy, leadership and organizational development. He serves on the boards of many companies as an independent director. He was associated with the Unilever Group of companies for over three decades and held several senior positions. He is an alumnus of IIT Kharagpur where he obtained a postgraduate diploma in Industrial Management, and was also trained by Tavistok School of Human Relations' faculty in the UK in individual and group development processes.

Why do you believe that money has become such an important aspect for employees today compared to the past? What advice would you give junior, middle and senior managers about the role of money?

I encourage younger employees to look at the learning potential, the climate that exists in the organization, the culture that prevails, and at whether the senior members of the management team have the propensity to nurture talent and to share their own experiences and wisdom with youngsters. So, I tend to encourage them to attach lower priority to money.

Having said that, young people now seek instant gratification. Their own tolerance levels to wait for better things to happen—which can be bought with money—is low. Therefore, if they suddenly set their eyes on a better car or a better apartment or an overseas holiday, then they want more money. So, they give money higher weightage over anything else professionally. They may listen to you about the value of training and having a nurturing environment, but there is a propensity for them to display different equations when it comes to comfort and lifestyle which can be bought with money.

So, if you were to do a comparative analysis, money has become more important today than it was for employees in the past?

I believe so. Individual differences will always be there, but predominantly, the joy seems to be in favouring the here and now, so money does have a premium. On campuses too, the tendency is to look at who is offering the best package. By and large, there is a 15–20 per cent increase in campus start-up salaries year on year, especially in the premier institutions.

What about senior and middle management employees?

When it comes to middle and senior management, I think money need not necessarily be the main consideration. It is a factor, yes, but there are other things as well. They are really looking at opportunities for career advancement, to move into larger and challenging roles, to stretch their leadership potential, as also other issues such as location.

Five Things to Remember about This Dilemma

1. Money is important. One must be compensated fairly for one's talents. The question of money is different across industries and companies. Every company has their own EVP. I remember, in Nokia, we used to say that you worked for the culture of the company and the love of the brand. The Nokia board would always ask me what premium we were getting for culture in the job market! Every industry and every company has a different compensation structure; one must understand that before comparing it with others.

2. Young people tend to switch jobs for small salary jumps. I do not agree with that approach. When you are in the first five years of your career, work in a company that multiplies your learning and capabilities. The rewards to be reaped in later years are fantastic. Frequent job hopping, which is observed to be the norm today, gets you short-term gain but gives you long-term pain.

3. Money has varying value throughout a career. For young people, it is about experiences; for middle managers, it is about building assets; and for senior managers, it is about children's education and providing for aged parents. Judge your need for money on the basis of the stage you are in your career. If you are good, money will follow you; however, if you have money, it doesn't automatically mean you are good. Try and be good at whatever you pursue—that will guarantee a good career and also good compensation.

4. I think people will value job security over salary and perks after COVID. That's why people are continuing to stay in companies where there has been a 20 per cent cut in salary and, in some cases, a cut in bonus for this year and no increment for the year. I think everyone agrees that some salary is better than no salary.

5. Be careful of taking on debt. Debt is about risk, and every individual has a different appetite for risk. You must choose risk wisely. Assumptions about future earnings and tenure in jobs are not the same now, unlike how they were in the past. Taking on too much debt will add stress to you and your family. It is simply not worth it. In the COVID phase, bank repayments have dropped by 200 basis points as a percentage of household expenditure.

Dilemma 2

Should I Do a Second MBA?

We live in a time of rapid change in business concepts and execution. Having witnessed varied revolutions, we have moved into the era of digitization, or what many refer to as Industry 4.0, with new terms such as IoT, blockchain, automation, etc., becoming common parlance. The sweeping waves of globalization are receding in many minds as most people feel that the phenomenon has benefited China but has hurt jobs in their own country. So many youngsters now think about doing an MBA. What is even more interesting is the other question that quite a few are asking—*Should I do a second MBA*?

This question may seem surprising to some. However, if one looks at the available data, there is a deeper school of thought behind this dilemma.

To better understand this, let's look at the structure of management education. India produces nearly 5,00,000 MBAs every year. One-fifth of them are employable according to many published sources. The quality of education is rather variable across business schools in India.

Youngsters opt to do an MBA to improve their financial status.

There are only 20 business schools in India where the starting salary post-placement is higher than the fees the student has paid for the two-year course. When they realize that they haven't got much out of studying in a second-tier business school, students think about pursuing another MBA in a better school. Towards this end, the priority now is to study at one of the top-ranked business schools in the world. These are expensive, costing an outlay of about $133,000 for a two-year course. In the past, students chose this route to migrate to a western country via an MBA. Visa rules and hiring patterns have changed and this is no longer an option now.

Today, competitive test prep coaching classes and consultants say they are getting more enquiries regarding a second MBA than ever before. Professionals armed with MBAs from Indian B-schools, including premier ones such as ISB (Indian School of Business) and the IIMs (Indian Institute of Management), are looking at international institutes and weighing their options, hoping it will help them leapfrog into the big league. The trend is prevalent across industries and sectors. You have area managers from FMCG (fast-moving consumer goods) companies, vice presidents from banking and senior managers from IT vying to go back to business school. At INSEAD, which offers a ten-month management programme, roughly 10 per cent of Indian students already hold MBA degrees from a business school back home, including the IIMs.

Reasons to go for a second MBA vary across the population but the motivations are largely the same. The first group is composed of management graduates who went to lower-rung business schools and are looking at better opportunities, roles and compensation. The second group, at the higher end of the spectrum, comprises professionals who harbour global ambitions or want to switch careers. Students also choose schools in Ireland because they obtain a time-bound work permit following the degree. Their choice is between a one-year executive MBA programme and a full-time two-year MBA programme.

Some Home Truths about the MBA

It's not hard to see why the first group is vying for a second MBA degree. Not so long ago, Indian B-schools earned the sharp rebuke of ASSOCHAM, which declared that, barring IIM graduates, 'only 7 per cent of the pass-outs are actually employable in India'. Things haven't gotten much better since. According to the India Skills Report 2019, the employability of MBA students has gone down from 41 per cent in 2014 to 36 per cent in 2019.

The three key variables in a good MBA course can be categorized thus:

a. The presence of rock star faculty in the institute (the best of the best in their fields) in the subject you want to major in
b. The quality of campus experience, i.e., student/peer group quality, extracurricular activities, industry interaction, etc.
c. The quality and pedigree of companies which recruit from the business school

These three variables are known to all the people running a business school, yet, somehow, in a majority of cases, the collaboration between the board, the faculty and the students doesn't come through. Business schools are more siloed than the most siloed organization. Which is why forging a united goal and having unity of purpose is all the more important.

What happens when these three factors do not work well in cohesion?

We see a dent in quality control, poor infrastructure, inadequate calibre in the faculty pool and resultant low-paying jobs through campus placement. Even global surveys have pointed out the gradual decline in the quality of management institutions and graduates in India. A report by Switzerland-based business school IMD saw India's ranking slip to fifty-three of the sixty-three countries ranked, down from twenty-nine in 2005. The data is worse.

If we look at the data, less than 50 per cent of students who graduated from 5,500 B-schools in 2016 found campus placement. The statistics reflected by ASSOCHAM are even bleaker when it comes to ROI (Return on Investment). 'On average, each student spent nearly 3 to 5 lakh rupees on a 2-year MBA programme; their monthly salary is a measly Rs 8000 to Rs 10,000, or 1–2 lakh rupees per annum.' These abysmal standards led to the closing down of over 250 B-schools in major cities. Even more are in the process of shutting down as Tier-II and Tier-III B-schools face yet another tough placement season with the slowdown in the economy.

Is There a Bright Spot?

It's not all bad news, though. The leading B-schools across India remain strong, with a range of recruiters visiting their campuses and good placements and job offers to show for it. Four Indian B-schools continue to be in the Top 50 of *FT*'s global rankings. ISB leads the pack at No. 24, followed by IIM Bangalore, IIM Ahmedabad and IIM Calcutta.

The IIM brand, as a whole, stands challenged. 'Even the quality of IIM/IIT students coming out now compared to the last 15 years has come down due to the quality of school education,' said the chamber. Part of this has to do with the opening of new IIMs, starting with IIM-Rohtak, and followed by ones in Ranchi, Raipur, Trichy, Kashipur, Udaipur, Nagpur and other cities. The new IIMs have not been able to match the standards of the older ones on several parameters, including the quality of faculty and students, infrastructure, as also the ability to attract top recruiters.

The IIM Bill has changed a lot of things from the past. Today, every IIM board comprises outstanding professionals

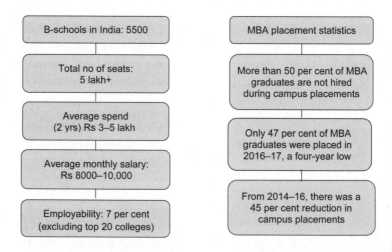

B-schools in India: 5500

Total no of seats: 5 lakh+

Average spend (2 yrs) Rs 3–5 lakh

Average monthly salary: Rs 8000–10,000

Employability: 7 per cent (excluding top 20 colleges)

MBA placement statistics

More than 50 per cent of MBA graduates are not hired during campus placements

Only 47 per cent of MBA graduates were placed in 2016–17, a four-year low

From 2014–16, there was a 45 per cent reduction in campus placements and eminent personalities and is empowered to make autonomous decisions in the best interests of the institute. I believe many of the new IIMs will do some path-breaking work.

Faculty shortage is a problem area for most Indian B-schools but the situation is worse in the new IIMs, partly due to their location. The best location for attracting faculty today is Bengaluru, whereas Ahmedabad and Kolkata fare poorly in this aspect. Business schools in Mumbai, such as SP Jain Institute of Management and Research, and Jamnalal Bajaj Institute of Management, have good credentials. Low salaries of faculty compound the problem, an aspect that is even more pronounced in lower-rung B-schools. Yet, the solution, as ASSOCHAM has prescribed, lies in re-training the faculty. 'The need to update and re-train faculty in emerging global business perspectives is practically absent in many B-schools, often making the course content redundant.' I feel that industry can play an important role in raising the bar when it comes to faculty capability through live projects and short-term assignments.

One approach for the applicant to take is to do their homework on finding out who are the permanent faculty and the adjunct faculty, and which campus gets very good visiting faculty or industry-led courses. From the Aditya Birla Group, we have run a 'Strategy into Action' course at SP Jain and IIM Udaipur, and are now planning to run it at MDI, Gurgaon, as well. This idea germinated in the 'Marketing in Practice' course run by Hindustan Lever in IIM Calcutta since 1994. I was the first speaker for that course in 1994, and I am happy to see it thrive to this day.

Will Automation Drive People into a Second MBA?

Automation is a challenge across economies. There is widespread agreement that many of the current skill sets in jobs which are repetitive in nature will be replaced by automation and employees will have to upskill. Young managers might be tempted to go for a first MBA or a second one if they realize that their skill set poses a challenge.

Here is a sampling of comments from second-MBA applicants:

> *'After graduating, I worked with BMW and then a PE-funded real estate development start-up. I was reasonably happy with my career progression, but over time, I increasingly felt that I wanted to move out of real estate and explore other industries in new geographies.'*
>
> —IIM graduate who went on to study at INSEAD

> *'I had no "real world" experience to apply my learning to. With work experience, I understood that there were many areas I needed to develop further. The second MBA gave me the opportunity to focus on some of these disciplines and made me a stronger business leader.'*
>
> —IIM graduate, who went on to Columbia Business School after stints in management consulting at PricewaterhouseCoopers

It is also about getting that breakthrough and putting one's career on an accelerated path. The Columbia Business School graduate is 'hoping to move into strategy consulting', an opportunity he says he would have found difficult to break into otherwise. While such ambitions drive the pursuit of a second MBA, career change is a big part of the motivation. INSEAD's Peter Zemsky says that about 80 per cent of their student body achieves career change—whether in function, industry or geography—after completing their MBA. This is very true of India too. About 50 per cent of MBAs change their job within the first year, simply because campus placement is like a lottery system and only some people strike gold and make it to the industry and company they truly want, or what is defined, on campus, as a 'dream job'.

Competing Globally

Another rationale underlying the second MBA is that industry practices evolve and there's pressure to not be left behind. Professionals with sector expertise go this route to update skills and competencies with niche courses. These are invariably new-age capabilities: from business models to data analytics and insights to customer management.

An MBA from an Indian B-school gives a good ROI but is less known globally. There's the perception that the Indian B-school branding is at best confined to the Asia-Pacific level. While IIM and ISB graduates do move out of the country, the numbers are still small, and this will need to multiply if the IIM brand is to have global reach and relevance in the future. I think the IIMs and their alumni have a lot more to do towards achieving this global objective.

Today, regardless of the size of the company, managers need to be equipped with global capabilities to perform across geographies. In such a scenario, an Ivy League school puts you on a global career trajectory, not just in terms of money but also exposure. These schools dominate global rankings, which are based on employment numbers, quality of faculty and diversity of the class. *FT*'s 2019 rankings throw up the same mix of names in the Top 10. Stanford and Harvard are the top two, followed by INSEAD, which is the highest-ranked MBA provider in Europe.

The dilemmas that crop up for Indian professionals in making this choice are aplenty. For those based in India, an international MBA opens up new horizons. Sometimes, Indian managers on international assignments may feel that, after a point, their progress is restricted if they don't upskill. Even managers who are earning good salaries may feel like they are stuck in their roles or that their field of work is too narrow and may grow obsolete. For others, it may be scaling their business or building one from scratch.

While candidates in Indian B-schools rely on the faculty and their projects and books for learning, peer learning is among the main draws at an international institute. Ivy League colleges often boast of their strong alumni network—rich resources that can be tapped into in the future. With average work experience standing at four to five years, diverse nationalities and profiles, the Ivy League school classroom becomes an attractive alternative investment.

India versus Abroad

The constant growth seen in overseas education expenditure does suggest that more Indians are opting to study abroad.

An estimate even puts the overall number of students across programmes at 0.53 million. Most second MBA aspirants prefer international shores for their 'back to school' plan. While exact numbers are difficult to come by, industry insiders peg them at around 1500 to 3000 per annum, roughly extrapolating from GMAT and GRE data.

For long, the USA has been the top destination for Indian students, but geographical preferences too are evolving. GMAC's data shows that the number of GMAT scores sent by Indians to US schools declined by 18.6 per cent from 2017 to 2018 testing years (1 July 2017 to 30 June 2018). Meanwhile, the number of Indians who sent GMAT scores to German schools rose by 29.5 per cent in the same period; for Canadian and European programmes, it rose over 15 per cent.

The dip in applicants to the US is not restricted to the Indian student community alone. According to a GMAC survey, 70 per cent of two-year, full-time MBA programmes in the US saw a decline in application volume in 2018. Harvard Business School saw a 4.5 per cent decline in applications, Stanford's Graduate School of Business a 4.6 per cent drop, and Wharton a 6.7 per cent slide.

There are two reasons for this trend. The first being that there are high-quality schools coming up in other regions, which is drawing students away. Shanghai-based CEIBS (China Europe International Business School) has risen to the fifth position, up from the eighth in 2018 in *FT* global rankings, making it the highest-placed Chinese school to date. The second reason is the fallout of rhetoric coming from the US administration and the strict visa regulations. Asia, led by China, needs more MBAs and these benefit from a local flavour.

Second MBA: An International Snapshot	
Pros/Benefits	**Cons/Risks**
Networking with people in related fields: With the average work experience at 4–5 years, peer learning is an important part of the programme. The diversity of the classroom adds to the discourse, boosting strategic thinking.	**Admission criteria:** Not all colleges accept applicants with an MBA degree. Even those that do ask you to justify taking the plunge a second time. The tricky part is doing it without discounting your previous experience.
International exposure required for global postings: An Ivy League degree means access to a global network and opportunities worldwide.	**Double the cost:** International MBA programmes are expensive. An overseas programme can cost up to Rs 85 lakh while one at ISB can cost up to Rs 37 lakh. Calculate the opportunity cost and ROI factors before deciding.
World-class faculty: Like your peers, the faculty you encounter in a good B-school are more experienced. Many are active in the industry and not just academia, which can open up some doors. Some are even considered leading thinkers in their respective fields, which helps build your skills.	**Salary and jobs:** It can be risky to do a second MBA to change your career trajectory. The remuneration expectations of a second-MBA grad are higher compared to first-timers. This can mean fewer options from the pool of companies.
Career change into unrelated fields and mid-career niche development: A second MBA overseas helps professionals who are looking for a career change while niche programmes can help mid-career professionals develop specific skills.	**Visa restrictions:** Increasing restrictions on visa/post-study stay options in countries such as the US can affect your chances after a degree.

Should You Take the Leap?

Immigration, visa issues, work permits will continue to drive the conversation when it comes to a global MBA degree. Despite its rising popularity, a second MBA is not for everyone. There are plenty of variables to consider in order to chart out how it fits in with your aspirations.

On the other hand, today, India does have the opportunities and the compensation for high-value talent.

Do you see yourself as a global leader or are you happy with a good position in India?

This is where you assess your long-term goals. If you see yourself in India for years to come, it may be a good idea to stick to the top-tier IIMs. If you are hoping to make a career switch to strategy consulting, investment banking or private equity with top firms such as McKinsey and Goldman Sachs, or get into a Silicon Valley company, then a second global MBA makes sense.

Are you prepared to devote at least two years to the entire process, including preparing for the GMAT, researching good schools, writing essays and then actually attending school?

There is going to be a significant chunk of time involved in the whole process. You have to devote time to this while pursuing your current job. Not all B-schools abroad accept candidates with a prior MBA degree. Dartmouth (Tuck), Haas

(UC Berkeley), Owen (Vanderbilt)—these are some of the top business schools in the US that do not admit applicants who have done an MBA before. Wharton and MIT Sloan are among the few who do. Almost all schools will ask you to address the elephant in the room: *Why a second MBA*? And what are you hoping to gain from it? You will have to build a strong case in your application, justifying the decision. That's besides narrowing down the schools, geography, debating a one-year or two-year course, and figuring out the money involved and means of funding it.

Can you achieve your career objectives with your current skills and brand? If not, what are your options, apart from another MBA, for faster growth?

Career change is one of the main draws for a second MBA, but it's a high-risk, high-reward situation. Like the B-school, you will have to convince prospective recruiters without discounting your previous degree. I cannot imagine many double MBAs doing that balancing act successfully. Speak to experienced consultants or alumni to understand the landscape for your target function and industry first. You may want to realistically evaluate what you are likely to get post-MBA, and whether there is, instead, merit in simply biding your time and learning the skills on the job. If you are going for that second MBA and planning to return to your current employer in a better role, ensure that you are not assuming things and have had the relevant discussions beforehand.

You will also need to evaluate if an executive MBA works out better for you. With a few exceptions, top B-schools do offer an Executive MBA programme and are usually quick to encourage older candidates to consider an EMBA programme where the pressures are not as demanding.

Are you ready for the financial liability that will come with a second MBA, especially one abroad?

An MBA degree doesn't come cheap. An MBA from a premier Indian business school costs between $25,000 to $33,000 for a two-year course. One from a top-five global B-school abroad costs about $110,000 to $116,000. The salary on graduating from a top-three IIM will be between $25,000 to $50,000, while that from a top-five global school will be about $166,000 to $225,000. So, in terms of multiplier, the Indian top-three business school pays back better. You must also calculate the broad opportunity cost you will bear when you are out of the workforce for a year or two. If you have a family to support, or have loans to pay off, this calculation is even more serious. According to a 2016 GMAC report, it takes about four years, on an average, for graduate business alumni to recoup their investment, depending on the programme.

Furthermore, please do not assume a quantum jump in salary following a second MBA. Your remuneration expectations are bound to be higher than your peers who are getting their first MBA. This can again mean job options and consequently, more risk. If you are from a tier-one MBA school already, chances are that you are doing well on the financial front. Should you go for a second MBA in that case? Introspection and cautious optimism are needed before you decide.

Advice on Doing a First MBA

On reading my manuscript, my editor asked me if I had any thoughts for people doing their first MBA. 'Is it worth it in today's world?' she asked. I give you my thoughts in case you are considering a first MBA:

1. Capitalism has been under fire in most countries, including America and the UK, traditional flag bearers of capitalism. As a direct result, there is some backlash as regards the MBA degree.
2. The backlash against capitalism comes from rising inequality, a winner-takes-all situation in the new digital industries, and the ratio of CEO salary to average salary paid going beyond hundred in many countries.
3. The commitment of capitalism to solve some of the challenges we face today—security, safety, ecology, sustainability—is under challenge.
4. Business schools have paid lip service to growing better human beings or more responsible leaders. The Harvard MBA oath developed by Nitin Nohria and gang after the global financial crisis has stayed exactly that—a verbal oath.
5. The business school and curriculum need a dramatic overhaul if they are to stay relevant to a future world. Till that happens, I think the MBA degree will be under challenge and scrutiny.

An MBA from a top-notch school will always be of value. However, that value is not lifelong; it will have diminishing returns if you are not constantly upskilling yourself or not performing well. All businesses want top-performing managers, not managers with top degrees. A top-class degree with below-average results is the worst combination in the business world.

I think we will see a higher emphasis on skills as opposed to degrees in the next decade. This will accelerate in a few industries to start with, before going mainstream. So, I predict that people will choose skills over degrees.

Kirthiga Reddy, partner, SoftBank Investment Advisers, and former managing director, Facebook India and South Asia

Kirthiga Reddy is an investing partner at SoftBank Investment Advisers (SBIA). She was earlier managing director, Facebook India and South Asia. She is co-founder of F7 seed fund. She served as chair, Stanford Business School Management Board, is a board member of Ballet and Beyond NYC, and serves on the board of directors for Collective Health and WeWork. She holds an MBA from Stanford University, where she graduated with highest honours as an Arjay Miller Scholar, an MS in computer engineering from Syracuse University and a BE in computer science from Marathwada University, India. She has been recognized as Fortune India's *'Most Powerful Women' and as* Fast Company's *'Most Creative People in Business'.*

You went and did an MBA after working for some time in R&D, and actually had a family to run, a course to do

and had a baby on its way. What prompted you to do an MBA and what factors came into the decision-making process? How difficult was it to manage the MBA?

As director of engineering at Silicon Graphics Inc (SGI), a $2 billion, 9000-plus people, high-performance computing company, my role involved business decisions about product directions and strategy. I began to consider doing an MBA to hone my business skills. It wasn't an easy decision. I was doing very well in my career, having risen through the ranks—from being an individual contributor to a second-level manager in six years. I analysed options like a part-time or executive MBA. Finally, my husband, Dev, said, 'Get the full experience of a two-year full-time MBA. Two years is nothing in a professional career of many decades.' It resonated! He also told me, 'It is better to regret having done something than to regret *not* having done something.'

We were expecting our first child, Ashna, a quarter into my MBA from Stanford Business School. She was born right after the first year. We partied more after she was born than before—she was up late anyway! She had 365 aunts and uncles—all my classmates. It wasn't easy but with tremendous support from my parents, husband and friends, I graduated as an Arjay Miller Scholar, top 10 per cent of the class.

A lot of technology employees want to do an MBA but don't take the plunge. Having been in technology roles plus customer-facing roles, what advice would you give them?

I firmly believe that one can do whatever one aspires to with or without an MBA. Mark Zuckerberg, CEO, Facebook, dropped out of the Harvard undergraduate programme. However, I want to acknowledge that such examples are exceptions and not the rule.

Personally, I look back on my MBA experience as transformative. It gave me the skills and the confidence that I could pursue any dream—no matter how big, no matter what field. It also opened doors faster to allow me to prove myself. In my final year of MBA, I saw a role at Good Technology, a mobile messaging start-up, that was compelling. It turned out that the CEO was from Stanford Business School and so was the hiring manager. It was the start of a very fulfilling next six years, leading to the acquisition by Motorola, and my move back to India to lead the Good Technology division in India.

My advice: If you start observing a growth opportunity from an MBA, lean into it. If you can afford it, don't sweat about a one- or two-year gap in career or income. It is better to regret having done something than to regret *not* having done something.

Bhavya Misra, HR director, PepsiCo

Bhavya finished her MBA from Management Development Institute (MDI) in 2007 and began her career with PepsiCo as Plant HR manager in Mumbai. After a brief stint with Bharti Retail, she returned to PepsiCo where she rose up the ranks to become HR director. She is currently based in Gurugram.

Why were you considering a second MBA? What was your motivation?

One of the things was the exposure I would get. Until then, my experience was restricted to HR, in India. I felt that with a second MBA I would learn concepts which might be different from what I had learnt here. It had been a while since my first MBA and I thought it was time to refresh my learning. So, learning and experience were the two motivations for considering a second MBA, internationally. I thought I would benefit from some peer-to-peer exposure and get new perspectives.

What made you drop the idea?

While I was really enthusiastic about doing it, a couple of factors made me drop the idea. I was already doing well in my career. I was working with PepsiCo and was growing. So, the first thing was the opportunity cost. How was the MBA going to add to my career? I also debated on whether the investment required was justified. That was the first thing.

Secondly, I was married at that point of time, but not for a long time. And though my husband and I decided that it would be okay if I went overseas since it was just a year, I weighed that against the real benefit of doing the MBA.

The third thing was, when I started doing research, I realized that even in all of the international MBA programmes, the average age (27–28 years) was much lower than mine. I was about thirty-two then. Some of my friends who had done their MBA from Ivy League colleges in the US told me that the quality of the discussions would not be what I was expecting because other students were younger. Their experience wouldn't be as rich because they would have worked for only about 3–5 years. Of course, there would be a range, but the overall peer value would not be there.

And that was one of the key reasons why I wanted to go for a second MBA—to meet a set of peers who would be able to add value. Of course, the curriculum and the professors are important, but when it comes to higher education, a lot of value you get is from your peers. So, I thought an executive programme might help me better than a second MBA.

As an HR professional, do you support the idea of a second MBA?

I do. Taking time out from professional commitments and investing a significant amount of time and money in upskilling says a lot about the person. I would take it pretty positively, but as I said, when I looked at my own situation, it didn't seem to fit in that well. I found alternatives that may work out better for others too.

People often go into a second MBA assuming that it would lead to a quantum jump in salary or a designation. Is it right to make these kinds of assumptions?

It depends. If you are specializing further in what you are already doing, it might help you fundamentally shift planes. But if you already have a number of years of work experience in a certain field and completely want to change function, then the experience will have value, but from a financial standpoint, I don't think it will fundamentally shift your plane. But more than the financial jump, an Ivy League degree has a huge significance when it comes to big roles in MNC organizations. So, this is good from a long-term career perspective.

How prevalent is this trend becoming in India currently?

I think people talk about it a lot, but I wouldn't say that it is very prevalent. In India, most people immediately get into an MBA after their undergraduate studies, without any work experience. And once they start working, a very small percentage of them, at least from what I've seen in my own network, decide to go for a second MBA.

Five Things to Remember about This Dilemma

1. You have to be clear about why you want to do a second MBA. Is it that your first MBA hasn't delivered to your

expectations? Is it that you want to work abroad, and so a second MBA from a global school gives you a better chance? Is it a question of reskilling yourself to do better as you hit middle management?

2. Not all global institutes accept professionals with an MBA degree. So, you have to pick the ones with a reputation and a proven set of top-notch companies that recruit from that campus. The quality of the campus experience is an important variable and you must dig deep into that aspect before you make the decision.

3. Calculate the broad opportunity costs before taking the plunge. The cost of a second MBA at a top-five business school varies from $110,000 to $116,000 for a two-year course. On top of that, you would have given up two years of current earnings. So, consider whether doing a second MBA is a wise decision financially.

4. The demand for MBA education is dropping if one sees the surrogate measures, such as GMAT applicants, and applications to top business schools. This is a combination of rising nationalism in the top ten countries of the world. So, doing a second MBA in the hope of working in another country has low probability.

5. In choosing a business school, whether for a first or second MBA, do your due diligence on the faculty of your topic, the campus experience and the type of companies that come to recruit on campus. I see people trending towards skill-based courses versus a full MBA, either a one-year or two-year course.

In summary, I am not a great believer in the theory that you must do a second MBA. It only works for a handful of people.

Dilemma 3

Living Apart

In this chapter, we talk about couples who stay apart for economic and career reasons. This could be for a short period of time, and in some cases, for longer duration. This dilemma is a bit more modern, having evolved only over the last decade. We do recognize the trend prevailing even in the past, though, when we look at Kerala, where the men, and sometimes the women too, moved to the Middle East in search of better opportunities while the rest of the family stayed behind in Kerala. Economic reality and the math involved are the sole reason behind this pattern of staying married but living apart.

The Indian family structure is changing. The perception of India as the land of giant joint family structures is no longer true; government data indicates entirely otherwise. In 2011, in urban India, 52.3 per cent of families were nuclear (husband, wife and unmarried children living together under one roof), whereas, in the same year, in rural India—hold your breath—the corresponding number stands so close at a whopping 52.1 per cent and the number of joint families stands at 16.1 per cent of households. Joint families showed much higher pooling of resources and offered immense benefits, including the fact that one's spouse didn't have to work to contribute to the joint family coffers.

On the other hand, we now have many couples in the nuclear family pattern looking out for some job or the other because they realize the need to maximize their economic potential. It starts out with both individuals working in the same town or city, then eventually opting to live separately for a period of time when some economic choice or the other forces their hand. Invariably, the choice is about a better opportunity for one of the partners or a transferable job that compels one or both to move. And this trend (of couples living apart) is on the rise in India.

In the West, there is even a special term for couples who are married but live apart. They are called LAT couples, which stands for 'Living Apart Together couples'. Studies vary on the numbers; a recent one pegs them at about 3 per cent of all 62 million married couples in the US. This increases to 9 per cent in the UK, where not only marriages but long-term partnerships are also taken into consideration. This is likely because distances in Britain are far lesser than those in the USA and every large city is just a few hours' drive away.

Three Big Reasons for People to Stay Married but Live Apart

1. Both people in a marriage or relationship have good jobs and feel they can do well in their careers. As a result,

when one person is transferred or lands a better job in another city, he/she decides to move.

2. School-going/college-going children are another factor. When one person finds a better opportunity but the family does not want to disrupt the children's education, they decide to live apart.

3. Thirdly, when one among the couple decides to study further and hence moves residence.

Companies try to accommodate this sort of thing, but it's difficult to handle. In today's context, more people are willing to give it a try because they stay connected on the Internet and any city in India is reachable within a couple of hours' flying time at most.

When Does One See This Trend—Is It Early in the Marriage or Later?

The nudge to stay apart yet together is felt during the initial years of a marriage. Studies show that the share of LAT couples is highest in the twenties and thirties, when careers are typically on the ascent, and the number dips as couples have kids and approach senior management and retirement.

It's technology that's a big saviour in such cases. The wide range of tools available for convenient interaction— video chatting, text and picture messaging, co-streaming sites—is how such couples try to make it work. Other factors, including access to low-cost airlines, easy availability of accommodation, more women in the workplace, also help accelerate LAT thinking.

What's Changed?

If you get down to the basics, migration for work is not a new phenomenon. The Indian Census of 2011 reveals that 454 million Indians (37 per cent) are now settled in a place different from their earlier residence. In 2001, this figure stood at 315 million. The majority of the women in this tally have migrated for marriage but 'work and employment' remains the top reason, mentioned by 30 million of the 140 million male migrants. This includes both blue-collar and contract workers in informal sectors facing the dilemma of livelihood and corporate executives chasing career growth. Data from the United Nations Department of Economic and Social Affairs shows India as the top source of the international migrant population—the country of origin of over 17.5 million immigrants, or 6.4 per cent of the global total, looking for better employment opportunities. So, the trend is prevalent both within and outside India.

What's changed then? As an Ernst & Young study puts it, the days of the passive 'trailing spouse' are over. The percentage of working partners is sharply increasing with generations. 'While 67 per cent of baby boomer partners are professionally active, this is 86 per cent with Gen X partners; and 90 per cent of Gen Y partners who will soon become the majority of mobile employees,' it says. The same argument applies to the education levels of partners, many of whom have earned postgraduate degrees or even PhDs, enabling them to independently decide the course of their careers. The old categorization, dividing partners into two groups—working and non-working—no longer represents ground realities.

Another factor mentioned earlier is that dual incomes have become more of a necessity than a choice. Often, income generated by one's partner is the key to sustain or even meet a certain lifestyle and ensure future reserves. 'If we focus specifically on the income of the partner, 56 per cent of partners report their income as "significant" or even "critical" (13 per cent), to sustain the family lifestyle,' says the EY report.

When it comes to international assignments, the situation gets trickier with more variables at play. A global survey by the Permits Foundation listed a lack of job opportunities for the spouse as a major mobility deterrent for senior executives. Expat rules in many countries, including India, are yet to fully factor in this element of business hiring. The decision for expat couples is compounded by practical relocation issues and cultural barriers, overall lifestyle and quality of living. Other challenges are good-quality education for children and concern for aged parents who cannot be taken along to the new country of posting.

Global Mobility

Yet, there's no denying that the number of mobile employees is on the rise. Having access to talent continues to be a challenge for CEOs and companies—a situation that drives mobility. Research firm Strategy Analytics predicts that 1.87 billion people will be mobile employees in the next 4 years, comprising 42.5 per cent of the total global workforce. It sees a larger number of mobile workers in Asia, given the changes in technology and a younger workforce.

This bodes well for millennials, who are more open to international assignments. Eighty per cent of them expect and want an overseas assignment during their career, according to PwC's Talent Mobility 2020 report. From which stems another dilemma—keeping up with their aspirations while mitigating costs. The solution? Companies are changing the nature of assignments. Traditional, fixed mid- and long-term assignments remain important, but only for senior management. HR managers acknowledge the shift—for managers or professionals, companies want mobility at a more affordable price. This translates to short and frequent business trips instead of assignments, short-term projects, or a work-from-anywhere policy.

Countries are getting tougher on expatriate appointments. Tightening trade and immigration policies is having an effect on the US as a destination as also the UK because of Brexit. Changes owing to heightened nationalism reflect in a BCG survey, which shows that the overall willingness to emigrate has dipped. About 57 per cent of all respondents in a 2018 survey said they would move to another country for work. While that's still a sizeable number, it is 7 percentage points lower than 2014, when it was 64 per cent. This will be a problem in countries where the local economy cannot provide enough opportunities for talented people.

There's much disparity among developed and developing nations, as is to be expected. Even the Chinese are now less inclined to emigrate, given that the country boasts of opportunities in many areas. India and Brazil, however, contradict the global trend. More than 90 per cent of Indians and 70 per cent of Brazilians say they would be willing to move to another country for the right job. There are four broad highlights that throw light on the single workers versus married/LAT situation in the BCG report. Single employees, men, employees without children, and younger workers are more likely to venture abroad. The results conform to expectations, but at the other end of this spectrum is the pack with experience and skills acquired over a good career.

The Need for a Support System

Companies are recognizing the need to manage this new scenario differently.

We can see many changes in the married/LAT universe. Until a few years ago, most employers only recognized legal spouses as beneficiaries of any support offered, but this has now broadened to reflect the wider gamut of relationships today, such as 'significant other', and so on. HR leaders and employers, too, are not in favour of splitting families. It's seen as a viable solution by only 6 per cent of employers in the EY survey. Over 77 per cent of employers see challenges and risks in destabilizing the family. Consequently, relocating partner support has evolved from lip service to well-thought-through programmes.

This has to do with the fact that mobile employees are no longer satisfied with merely the financial aspect of their international assignment; they also expect some form of support. Most employers offer this today, precipitated by the direct link between family well-being and success of an assignment. The data here speaks for itself.

- Close to 33 per cent of employers have increased partner support
- The most common reason for a failed assignment, mentioned by 71 per cent of corporations, is an unhappy and unintegrated partner in the host location

So, companies have to manage the family as a whole, as opposed to doling out a role for one person alone. Support programmes range from career and job search assistance, aimed at helping partners to work while abroad, to help with acclimatization. But keeping families together is not always possible, internationally or even domestically. Couples, as we have seen, might have to pick between a lucrative job offer and a traditional family ecosystem. In such situations, the priority is not to assist with the job search but to figure out work schedules, flexibility, fly-back support and monetary benefits, among other initiatives, to help couples make the hard choice. R.R. Nair's comments on the LAT trend are illuminating.

> If you are hiring someone co-located with their spouse, it may be worth checking out whether you are in a position to offer the responsibility in the same location at least in the first three-four years. But if you are uprooting them, then you will have deeper questions to ascertain—the key motivations and inclinations of the person in question; the adjustments required; whether the role warrants the person being co-located with the rest of the leadership team; whether they need to get back on the weekends and re-join on Monday; would the arrangement produce stress

and strain and have implications in terms of the quality of engagement with the role, etc. Having a conversation around the implications and the impact of those on the quality of deliverables is important. But the final call would be to leave it to the individual concerned.

There's stress and strain on relationships, no doubt, but technology gives couples the illusion of being together. LAT couples cook in tandem, eat the same meal, or watch the same movie in separate homes, with their smartphones or tablets near at hand. Some fly back and forth, or have video chats scheduled, so they don't see themselves as living separate lives. There are difficulties. Lack of meaningful time together, making it harder to create traditional family atmosphere for children. Constant running back and forth. Higher cost of living in keeping two houses and no time for socializing. But couples are perfecting what the *WSJ* calls 'the long-distance marriage that's built to last' as a way to advance their careers. It may not be for everyone, but it's an option more couples are considering in an evolving workspace.

I have observed many couples living apart. I have done the same myself for short bursts of time. It is never easy and I would not recommend it. I have seen the following patterns:

a. Couples get engaged and are living in two cities to start with. They are both in love and want to spend every weekend or every holiday together. As a senior manager, I have tried to be as accommodating as possible. I would sincerely believe it was a short-term phase where the couple needed support and I would find that concerned employees go that extra mile to do more when the organization supports them.

b. Couples graduate together from business school and land up in two different cities after they are married. Both feel they have a good thing going in their respective jobs and would like to continue for a few years to see what is possible.

c. Middle-level managers, after they have a child, have a support system in one city and are unwilling to give up that support when a new opportunity comes along. I have seen people manage this well, as things are more settled at middle-management level and the couple take a more balanced decision.

d. Senior managers live apart, because, by this time, they have provided for many of the family's comforts and are more at peace with this deliberate decision. They are also at a stage when the decision has fewer downsides and the family is more comfortable with the decision.

Priyanka Vijayakumar, entrepreneur, ex-head, Consumer Practices, Aditya Birla Fashion and Retail

Priyanka Vijayakumar graduated with an engineering degree from the National University of Singapore in 2009, following which she spent a few years in technology roles in Singapore, developing apps, among other things. After moving to India, she enrolled in an MBA programme at IIM Calcutta in 2013, and thereafter decided to enter the corporate world, joining the

Aditya Birla Group. After three years across corporate strategy and business development roles, she moved to Aditya Birla Fashion & Retail where she headed Consumer Practices.

Why did you and your husband choose to live separately in Delhi and Mumbai? Is it because you had two good jobs?

That was one of the main reasons. My husband was in a consulting role, and we always had a mental picture that it could involve a lot of travelling. Luckily, for a year and a half into our marriage, we lived together in Mumbai. But then he got a great opportunity to join a venture capital firm, which required him to shuttle between Delhi and Bangalore. I encouraged him to go ahead, in spite of the relocation. It was a very interesting, high-tech role, something that was obviously very close to his heart. In hindsight, I think it was a great decision.

Initially, he was required to live in Delhi because his team was there, but we had a conversation about both of us eventually moving to Bangalore because I have family there. Moving to Delhi would have been a huge change for me. Obviously, it would probably have made sense if I had moved with him, but I was only six months into my job. I was working with a fantastic manager and I wanted to learn and grow. So, I decided I would stay put and not move at that point of time.

As a young couple, when you decided to live separately, was it a big economic drain on you? How did you manage

some of the practical challenges involved in maintaining two homes?

For the first year, we managed it pretty easily. My husband's company had fly-back allowances as his home was in Mumbai. They were okay with him flying back and forth and even providing allowances for rent, etc., so company support was very forthcoming. But after that, we had to pay for ourselves to travel back and forth every weekend. That was not just an economic drain, it was emotionally and mentally draining as well.

Every weekend, we had to plan an outing in the most economical way possible, book tickets in advance, fly out on a Friday evening and return on Monday morning. So, we had to inform people in our teams in advance. When it came to doing basic chores related to banking formalities or investments, we had to do them only over the weekend when we were around each other. We had very little time to socialize and meet friends because the little time we had, we wanted to be around each other. And that continued for about one and a half years. So, yes, it was very draining.

You did this very early in your career and also in the second year of your marriage. Was it a good decision to do it so early?

In hindsight, that was the only time to do it. Currently, we don't have children, but once we do, it will become a lot more difficult to do something like this. It's important for both of us to have good careers. We have invested a lot of time to come to where we are at this point. The opportunities have come because of our efforts and ambition. So, our careers were something that we didn't really want to compromise on. In retrospect, the effort that went into making the long-distance partnership work was an experiment that needed to be carried out, and, practically, that was the only time to do it.

Now that you are living together again in Bangalore, if you had to do it again for a better career opportunity, would you be open to it, or is one experience enough?

I think I will let it be for now. We've just started settling down in Bangalore after one and a half years of being apart. If I had to do it again, I would need assurance from my company that they will bear some of the economic burden. Apart from that, the situation would have to be such that one of us would have to be in Bangalore because I have my family here. Plus, at this point of time in my life, I also want to think about starting my family, so I don't want to live apart from my husband. I think I wouldn't do it again for another ten years.

When you did do it though, was there pressure from your respective parents? How did you handle that?

There wasn't too much pressure. There were certain expectations though, because they were not aware that there would be a lot of travelling in such jobs. However, they managed, but we were emotionally drained. I think we caught on to that.

What were the moments when you felt the separation was just not worth it?

I think it happened every day. But I realized that it was for the greater good. Because we are two ambitious people. We don't just want jobs; we are looking at building careers. It is something we are very mindful of. That's what we would say to each other when we felt low about all this. In the beginning, we were excited but towards the end, half the time we were exhausted. Our social life was affected. We were saying no to friends all the time. At some point, it all became too much.

Vivek Gambhir, former MD and CEO, GCPL

Harvard-educated Vivek Gambhir moved to India in 2005 after working for twelve years at Bain & Co. in the US to set up their India operations. But he quit his consulting job as partner in Bain India in 2009 to join a client he was advising, the Godrej Group, as Chief Strategy Officer. At the time of the interview, Gambhir occupied the corner office at one of India's

largest FMCG companies, serving as MD and CEO of GCPL
(Godrej Consumer Products Limited).

What prompted you to stay separately from your family?

It was triggered by a job change. I was working for Bain &
Company at that time, and had moved to India after twenty
years in the US. I was to be based in Delhi to essentially
help start Bain's operations. I had moved in 2005, and this
was in about 2009. We had been in Delhi for almost four
years, and part of the reason to move to India, along with
the excitement of launching Bain's operations, was to be
close to my parents, who were living in Delhi at that time.
Then, I got this opportunity with Godrej. And Godrej, of
course, was based in Mumbai. The reason I was exploring
living separately from my family was because they had just
recently moved from the US. So, I decided to move alone to
Mumbai rather than disturb all of them.

Initially, we thought we would try it out for one year
and see how things worked. At that stage, we had two kids
and they were relatively young—my older daughter was
eight years old and my son was six years old. So we thought,
let's see how things pan out and assess the situation. Now it
has been ten years that I am doing the back and forth.

**Did you do it because it was Delhi and Mumbai? Would
you have done the same if was a different set of cities?**

More than the cities, I think the bigger driver was frequency
of flights. So long as enough flights were available between

the cities, I would have been city-agnostic. So, it could have been Delhi–Kolkata or Delhi–Bangalore and I think it would still have worked out. It wasn't done just because it was Mumbai, but obviously Delhi–Mumbai has the highest numbers of flights, so that definitely helped.

How often do you do this back and forth?

Typically, I spend Monday to Thursday in Mumbai, or if I am not in Mumbai, then somewhere internationally, because half the business runs outside India. I try working from home on Fridays in Delhi; we do have the Godrej office in Delhi as well but I don't go there. I do a lot of my thinking or long-term planning work from home itself. So, I have a fair amount of flexibility. I also try to see if I can work from Delhi on a Monday. So, there is no hard-and-fast rule as such.

How difficult is it to live separately and what sacrifices do you have to make? What's the logistical planning that goes into making this work?

I never looked at this as a sacrifice. This was an opportunity I was very excited about it. At the same time, I felt like I had responsibilities towards my family. So, I was trying to figure out—is there a way to strike a middle ground? Can I combine the best of both?

I think the critical requirement to live separately is that you need an absolutely amazing and supportive spouse.

I have a spouse, who during the last ten years, at certain points, de-prioritized her career. Now as our kids have grown older, she has gone back to working full-time, but she was essentially working part-time in the beginning. So, you need a spouse who is very flexible and supportive, and I have been very lucky to have Rupi, who has backed me in every decision.

The second thing is that you need an amazingly supportive team. The Godrej culture is one that focusses on results and outcomes. Facetime is not that important. There are other people who are doing this too—there is someone who is doing this between Singapore and Mumbai right now. Multiple people have done this between Delhi and Mumbai. But the culture is such that we say, let's focus on results and the impact. There was an extensive discussion about this in the beginning itself and the company said, as long as it doesn't interfere in the quality of your work, we don't really care where you live. Bear in mind that it doesn't work in every culture. But I end up going out of my way as well to make sure that my absence isn't felt when I am not here.

What typically happens is that, on the days I am in Mumbai, the hours are pretty long. I end up working from eight in the morning till eleven at night to be able to compensate for the days when I am not there. Second, when I am away, we manage with video conferencing and phone calls, etc. The company has been quite flexible— sometimes, when there is an in-person meeting required and I am not planning to be in Mumbai, I try to figure out if I can change my plans, or people change the date. So, the level of empathy is quite important; it is a two-way street.

I think the hardest challenge, as your kids grow older, is to figure out how you remain relevant in their life. Particularly when they become teenagers. So, there are a few things which I end up doing. One is, regardless of where I am, I wake them up every morning. I realize that we have to create these rituals to remain connected, particularly when kids get older and they get distracted with their day-to-day life. Every evening, I also try and do a video call with them. Occasionally, I also try to help them with their homework.

The other trade-off you have to make is that, typically on weekends, your family comes first. So, in terms of thinking about your social circle or what kind of social events you attend, you have to learn to be more selective and prioritize your kids and family more than anything else. I have realized that if you want a successful career and a happy family, then these are important trade-offs that you simply have to make.

Finally, what I realize is that my wife and I have grown far closer together. Because we know that we only have limited time over the weekends, we end up spending that time on quality things, and less on arguing or worrying about trivial things. But it does require a fair amount of effort, including prioritizing our time differently, creating certain rituals to be able to remain connected. It is not for everyone, but if you have a supportive spouse and a supportive set of team members, then it is definitely workable.

You said you've gotten closer to your wife, but are there any other distinct advantages of living separately?

I think it provides more focus. So, when I am at work for those 3–4 days, almost everything revolves around work. And when I am with my family during weekends, it's all about the family. So, in some ways, the separation ends up providing a much higher level of focus. I have been able to compartmentalize. Obviously, there are many downsides and concerns about being away from the family, but if one can work through this, then it is manageable.

In hindsight, do you think it's been worth it? And would you do it again?

It depends on the employer. With the Godrej Group, it has worked out well. So, I think context is very important—having a very supportive wife and a supportive employer is critical. If either of these are not there, and if the culture of the organization doesn't support it, then I won't recommend it.

How important is it to be flexible about location from a career progression standpoint? And empirically, what are some of the trends in India? Are employees

increasingly mobile and willing to relocate without their families?

It is still early days. I find that while there is a little bit of that happening, generally, it is still taking time to convince people to be more mobile. The problem compounds once people become more settled. Typically, a big challenge for mobility is when both spouses are working. If someone is very young, obviously they have no problem. But the minute people get married, things get complicated. Also, once people have kids, then the decision about social support in terms of child care, etc., becomes a bit of an issue. So, what I typically find is that, early on in their career, people are far more willing to do it, but later on, they hesitate to move, especially if their kids are in school, given how important that is for parents. But then mobility again becomes a lot easier once people's kids are in college or are much older. So typically, people who are forty-five or fifty-plus are far more willing to be mobile again.

Five Things to Remember about This Dilemma

1. Living apart is tough at any stage of your career. Couples who make the decision do so with the objective of maximizing one or both of the careers with an intention to be better off with the decision. Living apart takes a toll on personal relationships plus family bonds.

2. Affordable house rent, strong digital infrastructure, cost-effective video calls, and cheap airfares are making it easier for people to make this decision today, compared to the past. This is true for those living apart both domestically and internationally.

3. Living apart works best for senior managers because, by then, fundamentals are in place and it is a deliberate decision which is well thought through; also, the family has a choice and say in the decision.

4. A support system is crucial to the living apart decision. You should really think twice if you don't have a strong support system when you decide to live apart. The support system can be parents, in-laws, domestic help, siblings, etc.

5. Very few people can evaluate the return on this decision. It is a difficult decision to calculate any return. I don't think there is a correct way to do it, since there are more social dimensions to it and fewer economic dimensions because of which the decision was taken in the first place.

Dilemma 4

While Working Elsewhere, Rejoining a Previous Organization That You Had Quit

In India, attrition rates have always been high. They have been in double digits every year for the last decade. Industries such as retail and the BPO business have recorded the highest incidence. When people leave an organization, they always feel the grass is greener on the other side. But quickly enough, or just a couple of years down the line, they realize that things aren't as good as they imagined it to be. Then they have a decision to make—*Should I cut my losses and find another job, or should I go back to my old company*? This is the dilemma I will discuss in this chapter.

I can think of a few people who returned to their old company with success. Steve Jobs is a fine example; he left Apple and later returned to lead the technology giant on the road to greater success. T. Thomas, ex-chairman, Hindustan Lever, is another. He quit Hindustan Lever to join MRF, then came back to Hindustan Lever and went on to become chairman. Tarun Rai left JWT as a branch manager to work for Condé Nast; a few years later, he came back to head JWT as CEO.

How do companies react to this? What do they do when an ex-employee wants to return to the fold?

There was a time when hiring ex-employees was considered a risky strategy, largely due to an antiquated definition of loyalty. Today, employees leave a large company so as to experience life at a start-up, try a new industry, or even go back to business school for an advanced degree. Job-hopping is common. A Gallup study shows that six in ten millennials in the US are considering new opportunities. In India, 45 per cent of employees were looking to switch jobs in the year. LinkedIn says one in three millennials in India has held two jobs within the last five years.

The fact of the matter is that, today, it is an employee's market, not a company's market. So, employees have more choice and leverage. HR leaders are grappling with losing high performers, critical talent and experienced employees with expertise in new capability areas. This tussle for talent has tempered earlier reservations that came in the way of taking back ex-employees. It looks like the old adage applies here—*a known devil is better than an unknown angel.*

Companies are learning that it is prudent not only to welcome back on board ex-employees but also to keep in touch with them. From being ignored, or spoken of only in the past tense, or outright banned from all conversation, those who have moved on are now proudly embraced as alumni.

Companies are funding their alumni bodies and seeking their counsel on talent acquisition.

Talent is a scarce commodity and is possibly either No. 1 or No. 2 on a CEO's agenda. A global survey reckons that 76 per cent of businesses cite talent scarcity as a chronic concern. How about India?

Back home, over half (54 per cent) of HR leaders in Ranstad's 2016 survey said that talent continues to be a serious issue for corporate India. India's situation is slightly different from the developed world—we have a (stated) low unemployment rate, yet we are short on quality of talent. So, ours is a quality problem, not a quantity one, and as technology becomes more embedded in our lives and the demand for niche skills grows, this problem will grow more acute.

Boomerang employees—an expression for those who quit and later want to join back—is thus quickly becoming a talent pool HR managers cannot ignore and can well dip into. But it isn't as simple as it sounds. How does this work for the returning employee and the company?

Rejoining an organization puts additional questions on the table for the employee to answer. How do I reach out? How do I negotiate terms and conditions? What if I get rejected? How would my peers react? Would there be a feeling of ill-will? Is the culture the same as it was when I left? Will I be regarded as well as I was when I worked there? For companies, on the other hand, it's treading the fine line between whom to rehire and whom to reach out to when a critical position opens up.

Cost of Attrition Is High

A certain level of attrition is healthy for a company since it opens up pathways for others. It helps infuse new talent and rejuvenates an organization. The problem arises when the numbers go up. When I joined PepsiCo India, I remember we had a 20 per cent plus attrition rate in customer-facing jobs and a 30 per cent rate among distributors. This meant that only 15 per cent of geographies had continuity of both the salesperson and the distributor from one year to the other.

This is true across industries.

The millennials and Gen Zs have a propensity to get bored quickly and switch jobs as they have high expectations from their leaders. According to LinkedIn, half of Gen Z respondents were in their last job only for six months to one year, and 28 per cent of them are likely to change their job in less than a year. The reasons for this kind of job-hopping vary, but inadequate pay, poor work-life balance and lack of professional development crop up in all surveys. So, as an employee, if you quit for these reasons, then you are eating humble pie and going back to a place you blamed as inadequate for your talent.

The underlying fact to be noted here is that replacement costs can be high and the lost time may affect business. A Mercer study shows that 45 per cent of employers reported turnover costs of $10,000 per lost employee, while 20 per cent reported costs closer to $30,000. Even if you consider this a ball park number restricted to the US, there's no denying the high financial cost of attrition. This is US data, but I assure you that India has similar numbers to report. Let's take the example of a frontline, customer-facing employee who quits a company. It takes the replacement at least 3–6 months to get to know the customers and the policies and get accustomed to the growth patterns in place. You can compute the value in any company.

There's also the non-financial aspect in an organization to consider. I have seen that when anyone leaves, good or bad, other employees always feel that the company could have done more to hold the individual back. When a good person leaves, employees wonder whether there is something this person knows and they don't. A high turnover rate affects both the employee and the company. Any new employee undergoes a period of learning and adjustment, which can impact projects. A steadily dwindling workforce also affects morale and team dynamics in the office. HR leaders are no doubt paying attention to these numbers. According to a HireRight survey in 2018, almost half (47 per cent) of the businesses surveyed indicated they were investing in strategies

Top 3 Compensation Levers for Talent Retention

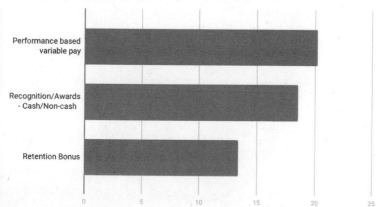

to retain their staff, which is more than double (22 per cent) as compared to the corresponding figures for 2017.

Consequently, every quarter, you see companies announce plans and bonuses to retain skilled employees, offer promotions and re-skilling opportunities. Money, as we have seen, is a powerful motivator here. A 2016 survey of Indian employees found that money could influence 21 per cent of the respondents into staying back, but it's not enough to stem the outflow. Employees are looking for strong leadership role models, with 19 per cent admitting that a good manager would keep them in their current role. Other important retention factors include overseas career opportunities and company culture, each cited in equal measure by 14 per cent of respondents.

These findings are in sync with the organizational changes millennials are bringing about in the workspace—focus on meaningful work, learning, business impact on the world, as well as blurring of hierarchies. The report mentions that 53

WHAT WOULD INFLUENCE YOU TO STAY WITH YOUR CURRENT EMPLOYER?

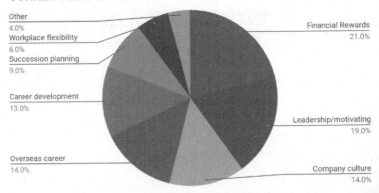

Other
4.0%
Workplace flexibility
6.0%
Succession planning
9.0%
Career development
13.0%
Overseas career
14.0%
Financial Rewards
21.0%
Leadership/motivating
19.0%
Company culture
14.0%

per cent of organizations are planning to invest in developing effective employee training programmes, up from 24 per cent in 2017. The focus is also on increasing the efficiency of HR processes, creating a positive corporate culture, flexibility and maximizing employee engagement.

Boomerang Employees

When looked at through the prism of arresting attrition, boomerang employees are a win-win. For starters, it's cost-effective to rehire ex-employees. You may have to offer them a higher salary than what you paid them when they left, but these employees take less time to hit the road running. An article in *Harvard Business Review* brings home the point: 'The facts are, it costs half as much to re-hire an ex-employee as it does to hire a brand new person; re-hires are 40 per cent more productive in their first quarter at work; and they tend to stay in the job longer. Research suggests that the average Fortune 500 company could save $12 million a year by actively recruiting alumni.'

I remember hiring back a few people after they had left the company. The best example is a manager named Sushanth. He left Nokia and joined a few friends to start a consulting firm. I did my best to convince him to stay. Six months later, he returned with no conditions. I have always offered a good employee the option to return should they choose to do so. I believe that both the HR team and the CEO have the best opportunity to hold back an employee who expresses the wish to quit; that's when they should spend time addressing his/her concerns. Once the employee bolts from the stable, it is so much more difficult to get him/her back.

With a boomerang employee, the risk of a costly mis-hire is also eliminated as finding the right fit is not guesswork. Even with all available modern-day tools designed to tell if a new employee will be a good culture fit, you already know how former employees fit in, both in the organization as well as with clients. If the employee has been gone for a while, they bring back with them a fresh perspective. In advancing their careers with the switch they made when they quit, they have acquired new skills, more leadership experience, even insights into how other companies handle different situations. This, I believe, is a win-win for both the employee and the organization.

Thus, many organizations are, as the *Harvard Business Review* article puts it, trying to 'cultivate ex-employees'. They are creating corporate alumni groups so they can stay connected. Microsoft, Citigroup, Dell, SAP, JP Morgan and Deloitte are but a few examples. One estimate says 8 per cent of the companies in the Fortune 1000 have some form of alumni programme, offering seminars and career-networking events, just like a university would. At Microsoft, roughly 15 per cent of the hires are reported to be boomerang employees. Rich Kaplan, general manager, Employee Services, tells *Quartz*: 'Maybe they went somewhere else because they thought the grass was greener on the other side, and they found out it was brown. But they only come back if you treat them with respect, and make sure they are fans and advocates.' This is something Harish Devarajan agrees on:

> People leave not just because they are unhappy with the company, but also because of circumstances. Somebody

needs to be in a particular city or somebody needs to relocate. Maybe they want to gain a different kind of experience and exposure that's not available in the current organization. These people, at a different point in time, might want to look at returning. If they have not left in bad taste and they were performing well, were people with potential, I don't see any reason why we should not welcome them back.

As an employee, it could truly be a case of the grass being brown. Maybe the new job or culture or pay is not what you expected. Perhaps switching jobs has given you insights into what's really valuable to you. Maybe the previous role was better after all. Or that, armed with new skills, you think you could make a better impact now in your previous organization. All of these are valid reasons to consider going back. But the decision also comes with the onus of explaining yourself to your ex-colleagues, rebuilding relationships, and maybe combating some office politics.

Of course, it falls to the HR leaders here need to make a distinction between whom to hire and whom to keep away. The answer lies simply in asking these questions: Are they the best person for the job? Did they have a good rapport with the team? Performance matters, but so does personality. You don't want to bring back into your organization someone who may hinder the productivity of the rest of your team.

Devarajan says:

One needs to be aware of two things. Do we see them as coming into a destination role, or do we see them continuing to grow and contribute? Second, what is the kind of reputation with which they went out and the reputation with which they will come back into the organization? Will it be welcomed as a positive addition, or be seen as a suspect decision? If the employee doesn't have much currency within the organization—not only from a management perspective but also from a people's point of view or a cultural/community perception of the individual—then the person is not going to be able to come and contribute on their return.

While you need to weigh the pros and cons in each case, alumni can also be the best source of referrals, helping companies fill crucial gaps. They are just as likely to influence outside opinions about an organization as current employees. Ultimately, the apt motto for HR leaders in this regard is to stay in touch with regret exits and be ready for when boomerang employees show up.

I would say, always leave a company with your head held high, having done good work and not in disrepute. People should feel bad that you are leaving; they shouldn't be happy to see you go.

If, however, your ex-company reaches out to you to rejoin, you must be clear on what your terms are. In PepsiCo, when we tried to get a sales head back, he quoted a very high price and left everyone with a bad aftertaste. So, rejecting the offer must be done as gracefully as possible.

Prakash Nedungadi, former group head, Consumer Insights and Brand Development, Aditya Birla Group

Prakash Nedungadi is a veteran business leader with nearly four decades of experience, spanning sectors ranging from FMCG, durables and fashion to B2B categories. After graduating from IIM Calcutta in 1982, he spent sixteen years at Hindustan Unilever, working across functions such as marketing, general management and supply chain. He then joined Gillette India as head of marketing in India before making a move to Madura Garments (an ABG company) as President and CEO. Nedungadi returned to Gillette three years later as business director for Middle East and Africa for the grooming business, handling sixty-nine countries. After brief stints at Procter & Gamble and The Teacher Foundation, he returned to head consumer insights and brand development at the group level for ABG, a role that he currently occupies.

What makes one leave a company and reconsider joining the same company again?

In a long career, you do business, you take up positions, but what you actually do is build relationships and you build a reputation. Your career takes you to various places, but the goodwill and the relationships that you build are what ultimately come back to you. So, when I left Madura and went back to Gillette, it was because I wanted to go back. All my career I had worked in a multinational setup, working in different countries, running different kinds of operations. I felt I needed to go back there because I got this opportunity to serve as a director for sixty-nine countries across the Middle East and Africa. And I thought that was a great opportunity. I was fascinated by that whole region. I had worked in Europe before, I had worked extensively in India, but I had never worked before in this part of the world.

So, it was not very difficult for them to say, 'Hey, why don't we get back and start working?' But it was not easy for me. Because you wonder how you're going to be seen, how you're going to be perceived by people. But I took a step back and thought about the experience I had gathered while I was away and how it would be adding value to the business. People welcomed me back as if I had never left. They were warm and friendly. It was a good feeling that I was wanted back, not just by people who wanted me for my skills and competence but everybody from my peers, to my juniors, to the staff. Everyone just seemed very happy that I had come back. And similarly, when I went back to ABG in 2012, again there was a bit of concern about how people would see me, but they were very happy.

So, you've had two stints at Gillette and two stints at ABG. How did the external world perceive this—your competitors, recruiters and the broader corporate ecosystem?

I don't think the external world is really that bothered about you. I think you should leave that thought aside. And even if it were, it should not be a point of consideration; the world will think whatever it wants to. And that is true whether you stay in a company, or move to another company, or come back to a company—everybody's got views but what is most important is what you think.

When you work in a company for a long time, you have a certain equity. When you go back, does that equity stay constant, or increase, or do you have to build it all over again?

That's the amazing thing. I thought that going back, I'd have to start from scratch. But that doesn't really happen. You come back very quickly to where you left off. People have a very clear idea of your strengths, of you as a person, whether they can trust you and you also have a very good sense of the way things work. So, compared to a newcomer, who comes in from outside, you have the strength of knowing the processes, the systems and the culture. And you settle down much, much faster. In fact, I settled down, in most cases, from day one. And after a week, I felt as if I had never left!

This was partly because of my approach. I checked how things were happening, what was similar, what had changed, and then adapted to that. I could understand the culture much faster than not only someone from outside, but also people within the system, because I'd seen it from inside, gone out and come back in, which allowed me to add my own insights and perspectives on the culture and the way things were done. But most importantly, it's the way people respond to you—whether they trust you and like you, whether they feel good about having you back. And that depends on how you good you were in the previous assignment, what relationships you built. That trust lasts a long time.

Rakesh Kumar, general manager, South Asia, SC Johnson

Rakesh Kumar graduated from IMT Ghaziabad and immediately joined ConAgra Foods as an area sales manager. He moved to PepsiCo as a trainee development manager before quitting to join the Subhiksha Group, an early retail chain. He then returned to PepsiCo and rose up the ranks to become sales director for Andhra Pradesh, Telangana and Karnataka. In 2016, he joined SC Johnson and is today the general manager for South Asia.

You left PepsiCo and went back. Was that a difficult decision and what made you do it?

Leaving PepsiCo was a difficult decision because, at that point of time, I was doing pretty well. I joined back because I didn't like the value systems of the company I had joined, the Subhiksha Group. As soon as I joined, I realized that something was not right over there. So, when PepsiCo called me back, it was an easy decision. Most people were happy to have me back. Since the company called me, they gave me the role and location I wanted and it all worked out pretty well.

When you leave a company, do you switch off completely or still keep in touch?

I was working in a very small unit—the Mumbai unit of PepsiCo. I kept in touch with the team and they kept in touch with me. We were operating directly in the marketplace, so I was almost running a mini factory with 250 people in the warehouse. It is a pretty intense business, so you develop close ties.

Now that you're in a managerial position, would you hire somebody who's left and wants to come back after a couple of years?

It's an easy decision when it's someone who has worked with you, under you, or somewhere in the ecosystem. There are a couple of people who worked with me at PepsiCo who have joined me here. Some I knew, some I didn't and have come through references, but it is easy to hire somebody who's already worked for you.

Sudhanshu Vats, former CEO, Viacom 18 Media, and CEO, Essel Propack

Sudhanshu Vats joined Hindustan Unilever after graduating from IIM Ahmedabad in 1991. Over a three-decade-long career, he has straddled industries as diverse as FMCG, oil and lubricants, and entertainment. Vats is among the few people who've spent more than twenty years (on two separate occasions) at Hindustan Unilever, managing businesses as diverse as food, detergents and personal care products. He has also had a stint with Castrol India. He currently serves as CEO of Viacom 18 Media.

You left Hindustan Lever, joined Castrol and went back to Hindustan Lever. What variables made you move out of HLL and then go back there?

I joined Lever in 1991 as a management trainee. At that time, they used to hire from campuses, and I was graduating from IIM Ahmedabad. In those days, there were four distinct entities in India—Hindustan Lever Ltd, Pond's India Ltd, Brooke Bond India Ltd and Lipton India Ltd—but recruitment was under the Unilever group of companies in India. I started out in Hindustan Lever. Through the 1990s, the different companies were merged and it became what it is now—Hindustan Unilever Ltd. Over that period of thirteen to fourteen years till 2004, when I stepped out, I had done home, personal care and foods. I had done sales, marketing and business assignments too. So, in a way, I felt I had done everything from the learning point of view. I was keen to climb another mountain.

That is why I wanted to look at a completely different industry category. And I chose lubricants and oils.

Also, at that point of time, I was in Bangalore. I was heading Lipton. I was fortunate to work very closely with Pepsi to roll out Lipton iced tea. But both my wife and I are career professionals—ours is a dual-career home. She didn't land a job of her choice in Bangalore. For her as well, Bombay opened up many more opportunities. So, it was a combination of these two which led to the decision.

The final straw for me was that Castrol had been acquired by BP in 2000. At that point of time, when I was hired by BP for the Castrol marketing head role, there was a desire that BP will play a bigger role in India. This was under NDA 1, the regime of Atal Bihari Vajpayee and Arun Shourie. They had a master plan for the oil sector, where ONGC, the upstream company, and Indian Oil, the downstream company, were to be merged into a mega oil company owned by the Government of India. The other oil marketing companies, especially the two big ones—BPCL and HPCL—were on the block. Other opportunities were available to get into fuel retailing and fuel retail marketing which was fascinating.

But why did you choose to leave Castrol and go back to HUL then?

Because when I joined, the elections happened, NDA 1 lost and UPA 1 came in. With this new government, it became increasingly clear that some of the BP plans would be put on the backburner. There were many discussions regarding other projects, and we were looking at various options, investments in green field projects, etc., to find a way out, but none of that worked. In that period, we relaunched the Castrol master brand and took it beyond just oil to liquid engineering. India was the first country to relaunch.

Meanwhile, I had a good bonding with Lever and they were always in touch. They asked if I was open to looking at Lever again. The opportunity they gave me was fascinating because I would head modern trade where we look at organized trade and the way Unilever trades with organized businesses, such as Walmart, TESCO, and in India, basically Big Bazaar and now D-Mart, etc.

How did your peer group react when you went back to HUL?

It was very peculiar when I went back to Unilever. It was uncommon for people to come back. Gopal Vittal got back after I did. But before that, there were very few people who had come back after leaving. The first response of many of my peers was—*This is not a great move; why the hell has he come back?* I was coming back after a few years, but it felt as if I were starting anew. So, it was quite interesting. You had to jostle for space and it was not easy.

Why do you think this was the peer reaction?

I think it is a bit of peer psychology. In large companies, when a person comes back again, you feel like it's fresh competition. Particularly in organizations where people have lifelong careers, you don't think beyond the company. But the moment you start thinking of your workplace as a ground where you can learn, then the world is a playing field. Then I think the mindset totally changes. Stepping out opens up your mind, and it helped me.

Is it a good idea to keep in touch with your older colleagues once you've quit?

Yes, I always believe in maintaining relationships. In Unilever, there is a huge concept of batches; the year in which you joined Unilever is your batch. There is a culture of friendship within the organization, which is not so common to see elsewhere. It's difficult to form deep friendships at work, but Unilever always allows you to do this. All of us who started out with Unilever, particularly in the late '80s and early '90s, owe a lot to the company. That gratitude always remains and I continue to remain in touch.

In your current role as CEO, under what conditions would you take back an employee who left you?

The critical thing when people step out of an organization is—*Who is the person that stepped out?* If his attitude and culture and value systems were good and if he was an effective manager, I think the new world is about the revolving door. There are no closed doors. Sometimes, people like to experiment and come back. Working externally, in a different company, a different sector, enriches you. You begin to appreciate many things which happen within your own organization. You appreciate this world and you are able to critique it in a much better way. Therefore, I will remain open to the right set of guys—what we call a regretted loss. The doors are always open for a regretted loss, a person who was doing very well and ideally should not have left you in the first place.

Five Things to Remember about This Dilemma

1. You must always bring your best to work every day. If you leave an organization, leave with your head held high and leave with a legacy. You might not want to go back to your old company but it's always good to have that as an option, since one never knows how careers shape up.

2. The reasons you leave a company are different from the reasons you join a company. As a returning employee, you will know exactly what you are going back for, and hence that aspect will not be a surprise.

3. If you plan to return to your old company, you have to think through all aspects of why you are going back, and how people and the system will react to your return.

4. Companies today encourage ex-employees to come back, as long as they are valuable. Companies keep a tab on ex-employees through the alumni network and actively court them. Some companies specify that they will not take back an employee who has quit twice.

5. If you go back to your old organization, then you need to give yourself time to stay and do well. There is no point in going back to an old company to quit soon once again. That will put your reputation at greater risk.

Dilemma 5

Should I Take a Sabbatical?

Every job is getting tougher and tougher, and we all need a break from work. The usual weekend break—either a Sunday, or a Saturday plus Sunday—is clearly not enough at times. Some employees at every level, typically in middle management, seek a sabbatical. Women tend to take a break for maternity, and that is not a sabbatical. A sabbatical is when you take a break either to re-energize yourself, or to go and study, or to travel and see the world.

Earlier, there was this notion that only women took sabbaticals. This isn't true anymore. I see a lot of men as well going that route. I was stunned the first time I saw this happen, when one of my male colleagues expressed the wish to opt for a sabbatical. I thought he was quitting the company and didn't want to tell us where he was going, until I recognized that he was quite tired and in need of rejuvenation.

The concept of the five-day workweek started in 1908 and hasn't changed, while the number of hours per week of what constitutes work might have changed. We see the move to a four-day week in some countries now. The jury will take time to decide if this four-day week is a good idea or not; we will hear about it in a year or two.

So, what exactly is a sabbatical?

A 'sabbatical' is a paid or unpaid, extended break from work.

Why do employees take a sabbatical?

The big reasons are:

a. They are tired and want a break to rejuvenate themselves. I think both the employee and employer stand to benefit from this sabbatical. No company wants a case of burnout at work, where the individual's productivity will be close to zero.

b. They want a break to take care of an important aspect relating to their kids—either their development or a crucial year at school. This is an important need, especially when kids are in significant school years, have board exams coming up, and so on.

c. They take a break to care for their parents. This is noble. I remember Mohit Raina (currently CMO, Domino's) taking a sabbatical when he was leading innovation at PepsiCo, to look after his ailing father in Jamshedpur.

d. They take a break to pursue a serious hobby—be it photography, writing a book, mountain climbing, etc. One of my friends in a senior role took a break to go to the Mount Everest base camp with her daughter. This needed preparation, and of course, the time required for the climb up and down to base camp.

e.   They want to leave a company, re-skill themselves, and get back to another industry. One of my family friends is doing this right now; he has travelled to Argentina, taken a digital course at IIM Bangalore, and is re-evaluating which industry he wants to go into next.

Do companies benefit when an employee takes a sabbatical? Companies rarely plan a sabbatical for an employee; the only time I have seen sabbaticals arranged for an employee is when senior managers take up a new role. I have seen companies send senior managers to an advanced management programme in the US before they are moved into a new role. This gives the senior manager a short tutorial on new management concepts as well as a break from the daily grind at work.

Employees are not comfortable asking for a sabbatical or even approaching it at this point. This is true in all countries where the average work week is more than seventy hours. Somehow, such societies are not encouraging of this option. On the other hand, West European countries do encourage people to go in for a sabbatical. I remember the number of Nokia managers who would take one in Finland. I didn't hear of too many doing the same either in China or in the US, though.

Many employees fear that taking a sabbatical will hurt their career prospects. According to a research, 21 per cent thought taking time off could make them less employable. An earlier survey by London Business School found that 70 per cent of women fear taking a career break, whether it is to have children, to travel, or to study. Employees feel that, in many companies, out of sight means out of mind.

History of the Sabbatical

The idea of taking an extended break dates back to the late 1800s, when Harvard University began offering extended paid leave to professors. By the 1920s, the practice mushroomed, with as many as fifty universities offering similar programmes, although it remained restricted to academic circles for a long time. Slowly but steadily, it's becoming a sought-after benefit offered by employers, a marketable tool for recruiting purposes. According to a survey from the Society for Human Resource Management in the US, 11 per cent of employers offered unpaid sabbaticals and 5 per cent gave paid sabbaticals. 'That's a significant gain from 1977, when McDonald's instituted what was arguably the first corporate sabbatical programme in the United States,' says the *Harvard Business Review*. True, but the numbers remain range-bound in the US as the option is offered to select, long-standing employees. This is one benefit, though, that more millennials want across geographies. These days, many millennials feel stressed in their jobs and are seeking a sabbatical.

In an Opodo survey—conducted across eight countries (UK, Germany, France, USA, Sweden, Italy, Portugal and Spain)—71 per cent of respondents said they would consider taking a sabbatical if it were an option offered by the company. At 78 per cent, it was the millennials expressing a lot of interest. For a generation that has taken over the workforce and put its own stamp on things, sabbaticals align with millennial aspirations. They want to travel more, lend a hand to social causes, and have different experiences under their belt. An extended break offers them the leeway to chase these passions. So much so that in the absence of dedicated sabbatical programmes, employees are taking unpaid leave for months to de-stress, pursue their passions and engage with community projects.

One school of thought explored by Barrett and Linda Sharkey in *The Future-Proof Workplace* is that retirement will become a series of sabbaticals. They believe the future will involve periods of work that fund a sabbatical, followed by a return to work to refill the bank account for the next sabbatical. Far-flung hypothesis or not, more companies are giving employees the opportunity to take a break. Nearly one-fourth of Fortune 100's 'Best Companies to Work For' offer sabbaticals, some dedicatedly for community development and volunteering programmes.

There are no separate statistics available for India, but HR consultants deem it a trend that's fast catching on, especially in the last five years. A lot of them are leave-without-pay policies offered to employees who have strong performance records. You see them across administrative services, government, PSUs, ITeS companies predominantly; some, like their overseas counterparts, are volunteer sabbaticals. SAP allows Indian employees to take unpaid leave of up to two years to explore an entrepreneurial venture during their career break.

It's not just talent crisis and millennial demands that are driving these changes in the workforce. While the type (paid or unpaid), length (weeks or months) and other details vary, research suggests that the upward trend in sabbaticals owes to two primary factors—the employee aspect and the business one. When researchers surveyed sixty-one leaders from five different non-profit organizations that offer sabbatical programmes, a majority said that the time away helped them 'think out of the box' and come up with new ideas. Interestingly, they said it helped foster better relationships with the board of directors. Importantly, the study said, 'a sabbatical can be a relatively inexpensive but highly productive, capacity-building tool that yields measurable results'.

The Benefit of Sabbaticals

Compellingly, sabbaticals are a way to beat attrition. Studies show there's an acute need for extended breaks now when millennials, over and above other tags they attract, are also being called the 'burnout generation'. A US-based study says that employees who are highly engaged in their work also feel exhausted and ready to leave their organizations. Lack of engagement, boredom and disaffection are seen as leading causes of employee turnover, but stress not so much. The study finds that companies, in fact, risk losing some of their motivated and hardworking employees due to high stress and burnout—a symptom of what it calls the 'darker side' of workplace engagement.

This is especially true for leaders. The demands of leadership make intellectual, emotional, creative, and even physical burnout all too common among executives. Multiple surveys attest to this fallout percolating right down the pyramid. Three-quarters of employed Americans say they would like to take an extended break, with over half (53 per cent) citing the opportunity to escape the stress of working life. Stress (49 per cent), mental health improvement (41 per cent) and physical health improvement (35 per cent) were the top three reasons in the Opodo survey too.

An extended break and complete detachment from work helps alleviate this stress. Employees who take work sabbaticals say that they return to work feeling more inspired and less competitive. The space to reflect, time to travel, the opportunity to focus on personal goals—all contribute significantly to employee wellness. In academic circles, sabbaticals often involve engaging in research. Taking time off to learn a new skill can be beneficial to meeting long-term career goals too. As can social and volunteer work. There are personal stories galore of how a closer look at social issues has expanded vision or given rise to enterprises.

Often, though, a sabbatical can be driven by personal reasons, ranging from health to family commitments to emergencies. While companies are expanding maternity leave, flexible working options, some even introducing paternity and adoption leave, a lot still remains to be done.

Moreover, with family structures changing, we have dual-income families, LAT couples, single parents, who need to balance demands with or without a support system. Are companies prepared to understand their dilemmas? Vani Dandia, an independent business consultant, shares her thoughts as a single mother:

> Day-care facilities in office aside, one needs emotional support and understanding. For example, one's boss must understand that outstation travel must be minimized, that meetings must not overrun to late evenings, or that logging in from home isn't always possible.

Without this level of understanding, a sabbatical becomes the only way out from constantly juggling the demands of office and family. But even this doesn't come easy. It impacts women more than men. 'Women feel more negative consequences when they take leave: 20 per cent of women who've taken a leave say it negatively impacted their career, compared to 10 per cent of men. Women are also twice as likely to say it had a negative effect on their financial well-being,' says a McKinsey survey on working women. It may be specific to the US but it points to a larger trend—a career break for women brings in unique challenges. In 2017, a World Bank paper found that 'having a young child in the home impacts a mother's employment'. This widens the gender disparity in the workspace. Sabbaticals, fortified with assurances of re-joining the workspace, and return-to-work programmes are essential to close this gap.

It Makes Business Sense

At the very least, sabbaticals help stress-test the organizational chart. A brief sabbatical allows companies to see if they could survive unexpected employee departure. Having people rotate out for an extended period of time is one way to know how robust the team is for real. It's a dilemma to figure out how and who would look after their work, but it allows aspiring employees to take on more leadership roles and helps in succession planning. Staff members end up learning new skills and taking on new responsibilities. The capacity of the second tier of leadership is thus created, and on returning, the executive can then delegate more responsibilities and decisions.

Another issue that surfaces is: How will the employee's job shape up following a sabbatical? One challenge with a long break, say six months, is to accommodate the employee in a role which is commensurate with his/her capabilities. It's best to have a discussion beforehand. According to the non-profit study, cited by the *Harvard Business Review*, researchers found that 'the majority of leaders surveyed said that the interim leaders were more effective and responsible when the sabbatical takers returned. Many even reported that those interim leaders continued some responsibilities and made the overall leader-subordinate relationship more collaborative.'

Of course, restructuring roles works differently in different organizations, and that's something to be figured out, but sabbaticals do strengthen governance. Organizations also reported having much more confidence in their succession planning, since they were able to try out the role with the interim leaders. In some cases, 'the sabbatical helped make clear to the organization that the person who acted as the interim executive director was the right choice,' said the study. 'One group did a national search, but hired the deputy director who had acted as the interim because they had seen her leadership in action. Another organization had the opposite experience, where both the awardee and the interim mutually decided that the interim was not the right fit to succeed. The sabbatical process, in essence, allowed this organization to bench test a candidate for a new role.'

Yes, despite the benefits, for employers, there is the obvious cost factor involved. Someone is to be hired/ arranged to take that employee's place in his/her absence. In some cases, existing employees need to cover more functions. There could be hidden costs associated with a sabbatical, such as health insurance and accident cover. Moreover, the burden of funding a social sabbatical falls entirely on companies and that may not be cost-effective. For the employee, a sabbatical can create a financial setback. For someone with financial obligations, such as house/vehicle EMIs, credit card dues, loans, and a family to support, a career break can often be difficult unless it is a paid one. Even without any serious obligations, professionals need to ensure that they have adequate savings that will support them, or that they have some sort of familial backup. If the HR policies of the organization or sector are not encouraging of sabbaticals, it can cause career setbacks.

Small organizations may not have the elbow room required for a successful sabbatical programme. In such situations, companies can work out a partially paid or no-pay sabbatical. Not every employee wants to go on a six-month or one-year break. If planned properly, an employee's sabbatical will not impact work. In fact, it will work as a motivator and an engagement factor for other performers. For there's no denying that it is a good employee retention tool. Asked whether their sabbatical had influenced their decision to stay in a job longer than previously projected, a third of those asked said yes.

Pavitra Singh, CHRO, PepsiCo, India

Pavitra Singh started her career in 2001 with American Express in Gurgaon after completing her MBA in HR from the University of Pune. After a brief stint at Fair Issac in Bangalore, she joined PepsiCo as senior manager, Talent Acquisition, in 2006. At PepsiCo, she's risen up the ranks through diverse roles in capability building, organization design, diversity and inclusion, talent acquisition and employer branding in national and global roles.

You took a sabbatical in 2012. What prompted this move?

I had moved into a leadership role and was heading HR for the foods business of PepsiCo. I had just been promoted and was doing quite well. In 2012, I was already into the role for about a year, and it involved a lot of travelling. At that same time, my husband had also moved to a different organization and he had to travel a lot as well. Our daughter, Niharika, was five years old. She was just about to get into Class 1. Suddenly, her world changed, going from seeing both of us on a regular basis to feeling that neither of us was available. At that point, we didn't realize the impact, but it started showing through things such as her not wanting to go to school, some anxiety and so on.

We then went to doctors and teachers to find out what was happening, but I realized that it was our not being there that was affecting her. She just wanted a sense of security. That's when the penny dropped for me. So, one fine day, I just came back home and said to myself—nothing else is worth it, and I have to take a call about what to do. I just sent out an email to my manager and the HR head saying that I wanted to quit.

Typically, this is what happened to women. A lot of them reached a crossroads and, without thinking or talking to anybody, they took an impulsive, emotional decision. I knew at the back of my mind that I was in a senior leadership position, doing fantastically well. I battled several dilemmas and had thoughts about what to do, how to balance things, etc., but I was too afraid to bring them up or talk to anybody. A sabbatical was not the norm at that point of time. And that is what led to the impulsive decision to resign. It was a big shock to both my managers—they sat me down and we had a conversation. They said they understood what was happening with my daughter and they respected that, but told me not to quit and take a sabbatical instead, so that I could have a return ticket.

That moment was one of the biggest learnings for me—you need role models in your life who will help you and show you the way when you don't know what to do. And these role models happened to be my managers. Often, women don't have a sane voice telling them—it's okay, this will pass. Because you are dealing with so many emotions, your ecosystem—which is your family, your extended family—is putting pressure, and you are literally cornered.

As a senior HR professional, what are some of the reasons people take sabbaticals?

At one point of time, a lot of women were taking sabbaticals for childcare. But after I took a sabbatical, there were four men in my organization who took a break. It was like, *If she could do it at that level without thinking about the consequences to her career, why can't we?* I had many people ask me if it was okay to go ahead and do it. And people took sabbaticals for so many different reasons. The reasons were no longer only child care, and it was not something only for women but men too. One had an ailing father and had to take care of him; another wanted to explore if he could pursue studies overseas, the third said that he just wanted to take a break and travel. I think the fourth said that he would like to try his hand at entrepreneurship. So, some of these issues are very gender-agnostic. It is no longer a woman who has to take care of ailing parents; men do that too. Or with millennials, these are youngsters who have had enough, have worked very hard for the last 7–8 years, and just want to take a break and see what else life has to offer.

How is this trend of more men taking sabbaticals viewed by their peer group? Is this something which is frowned

upon or encouraged, because there are costs attached to it, both tangible and intangible?

As an organization, we have evolved. So, sabbaticals went from being just this women's thing to four men taking it together. Those numbers changed the whole equation; suddenly, it became okay to do it. Perhaps, if it was just one person who had done it, there would have been more questions.

From an industry perspective, not from a PepsiCo perspective, is this a wider trend?

No, I have spoken to many women at different fora, and I find that every organization is at a very different maturity level when you talk about diversity and inclusion policies. With sabbaticals, I don't think most organizations see that there are times when you need to dial down and there are times when you have to dial up. And it happens to both men and women. A lot of people come and tell me that if I take a sabbatical, my career is gone, so it is still considered a taboo. And I have seen that women are far more insecure about these things, because there are biases and women don't have the confidence to do it. Which is why I feel that organizations and role models play a very important role in this journey.

So, given that we are at different stages of maturity when it comes to how companies look at this issue, as

an HR person, would you still advise people to take a sabbatical?

Honestly, it depends on the phase of life you are in and what it demands from you. I would advise people to take a sabbatical, yes. The fact that people are even having this conversation is a way forward. Everyone goes through different phases, dilemmas and challenges in life and just by having a conversation with them during that time and saying 'Don't quit, go on a sabbatical', we've been able to stop 4–5 individuals, especially women, from resigning. Why do you think we have a leaky pipeline? You hire women, but during different phases, you see them dropping out. So, it is a great strategy to retain people because they all go through phases in life, and that's when they need support and someone telling them that it is okay.

As an HR professional, what's a good length for a sabbatical and what does it depend on?

There are no rules. At the end of the day, when I look at you coming in to work, I want you to be charged and happy with what you are doing. If a part of you is not engaged or totally into it, then there is something wrong. It could be because of issues you are facing at home, or the stage you are in, or because you need to do something else. Or you just need to rejuvenate—we see a lot of that in corporate spaces; there is too much of a burnout. There is no point hanging around and not being productive. If that is the situation, you should go ahead and take time off because, otherwise, you are not doing justice to yourself or to the organization.

I have felt that, at some point in time, everyone should take that break. Because you are in a pressure cooker most of the times, and you are grappling with multiple things. But not everyone needs to take a sabbatical; people find different ways of venting out, be it extracurricular activities or other things. But if this is your way, so be it. For me, that is more important than the length of the break.

When you are on your sabbatical, should you keep in touch, update yourself on what's happening at work, or cut off completely?

It is a personal choice. Different people do it differently. For me, I wanted to cut off, focus on something else, and did not want to carry any baggage, because you do get sucked in. So, during my sabbatical, I had compartmentalized things entirely. But for someone else, they might still want to keep in touch to know what is happening. My advice is that if you have taken a sabbatical, do it for a particular purpose, and go ahead and fulfil that. But you can have a mentor with whom you can connect and bounce off ideas every now and then.

Do you need support both personally and professionally during a sabbatical?

Yes. At the end of the day, an overall culture of support is what you need. My organization supported me. Not once did they question or even try to convince me otherwise. They were supportive because they genuinely felt it. I was lucky because, a lot of times, the culture is basically your manager, or the immediate ecosystem is. So, you might have the best policies, but you don't see them getting executed because the immediate ecosystem is not supportive. And it requires something like this to get embedded across different levels. So, everyone has a role to play—culture, HR, etc.

Ruchika Gupta, AVP, marcomm, Luminous Power Technologies

Ruchika Gupta passed out of NMIMS in 1997 with a degree in advertising and communications. She started her career with an advertising agency before assuming a role at Nestlé India as consumer insights manager. She spent over seven years in various roles at Nokia, had stints with Microsoft and Firefly Milward Brown, before moving to Luminous Power as AVP, marcomm. As a marketing professional, she has, over the last twenty years, straddled numerous functions, including brand transformation, brand and category management, app marketing, retail marketing, digital marketing, advertising, brand planning, PR, customer research and market strategy.

You took a sabbatical after your stint with Nokia. What prompted you to take one?

When I took that sabbatical, I was seven-odd years into my stint with Nokia. The only role that I wanted was taken up by someone else and it wasn't going to open again for another couple of years. Also, I had been working for close to fifteen years and wanted both a change of job and a break just to recharge myself more than anything else. At the same time, I was getting married and wanted to set up a new house. So, it was the perfect time to take a sabbatical before applying elsewhere. I didn't think of it as a long-term sabbatical at any point of time. The intent was that I was going to take a break, and once I was ready, I would return to the corporate world in a role that I wanted to do.

In what ways did this sabbatical help you?

It lasted about six months. It helped me get clarity on the fact that I was not meant to do things on my own. Before taking the sabbatical, I had toyed around with the idea of becoming a marketing consultant. I did a few projects with other consultants to figure out if I wanted to do this in the long term. But one of the best things that happened was that the sabbatical told me I was not very good at business development and not comfortable reaching out to the friends I have made in the corporate world for business. So, in some sense, it gave me clarity of purpose and told me what my skill sets were.

What are some anxieties and insecurities you had when you were on a sabbatical? Did you go through a phase where you were wondering whether this was the right thing to do?

Yes, absolutely. This anxiety struck me after about 3–4 months and I was ready to go back to work. I started reaching out to recruiters but realized that it wasn't necessarily going to be a cake-walk in terms of finding the job that I wanted to do. So, the fact that it could take me many more trials was cause for huge anxiety. Because there wasn't a huge gap in the market that I could just step in and fill. Marketing profiles were a dime a dozen. Even with fifteen years' experience, it wasn't a walk in the park.

Did your sabbatical allow you to further non-work-related interests and obligations?

It did. I finally joined an art class, something I had wanted to do for a very long time. I got to travel, and I definitely got a lot more time to spend with my family. In fact, coincidentally, my father was hospitalized during that time.

He had open heart surgery in Bangalore, and I was able to spend a whole month with him at that time.

How does a career woman decide when it is time to have a child? What variables do you consider?

I came back from my sabbatical, was head-hunted by someone from Nokia, and joined Microsoft. Soon after I joined, I realized that I was expecting. The good bit was, it was an individual contributor role, unlike the hectic team role that I handled earlier. So, it allowed me to work at my own pace. Also, Microsoft is extremely supportive. And my stakeholders were scattered all over the country, so for me the regular nine-to-five rules didn't apply.

Apart from your personal experience, what variables weigh on a woman's mind when she considers having a baby?

I have actually been counselling a lot of women over the years to not take a child break unless critically required. With the six-month rule coming in, it has become much easier for women, so that has been a huge boon. But in my experience, there are many women who took a break and then struggled to find their way back into roles they were happy with. Even in my own case, I took on an individual contributor role and moved to Milward Brown in a flexi-role. These moves were governed by the fact that I was a new mother and needed to be around my child. Physical proximity was important because I didn't have the support system of in-laws or parents at home and the choice was purely between day care or this.

What are some of the basic benefits that women must expect from an employer when it comes to maternity leave and why?

From an employer perspective, it's important to respect maternity leave. A lot of women I know are scared to take leave before delivery because the rules usually state that maternity leave is counted from the date of delivery onwards. But it is actually during the last few weeks of your pregnancy when you need rest. I have seen women in my team, and across organizations, saving up leaves and finding themselves in a dilemma during those last weeks about whether or not they should take their leave, even though I see them physically struggling. I genuinely think pre-delivery support for 2–3 weeks in terms of work from home or flexi-timing or something like that should be arranged by the company. I think it is equally necessary when they resume work, to not expect them to be full-timers from day one.

What are some of the anxieties women have, with respect to their career, when they are on maternity leave?

I have seen women saying they will lose out on promotion. I have had conversations about lost opportunities, where women missed projects because they were in a timeframe where they would be out of action. In fact, I have seen a couple of incidents where at least three women I know delayed telling their organizations about their pregnancy because of the fear of losing out on a project.

Post-delivery, how difficult is it to manage work and career, particularly in the first few years?

Unfortunately, we are not a very professionally organized 'day-care country', unlike the UK and US, where my friends have managed it seamlessly. In India, the support system that you have is not the most professional kind, even if you opt for the most highly paid option available. The family support system, unfortunately, is again blank in terms of that maturity or understanding. I still haven't heard of too many men taking their paternal leave or doing the same kind of flexi-work to support their wives. So, the constant guilt they carry affects a lot of women. The guilt about having to run back home, ignoring their duties as a mother. I worked between Microsoft and Milward Brown, who were extremely supportive about the whole flexi-work idea, but I had to take a huge pay cut to be able to afford that kind of flexibility, and it took me five years to recover and move back to the level I was at.

Apart from flexi-timings, what kind of infrastructural support can organizations extend to pregnant women?

I have heard of some organizations building crèches, but that isn't common at all. If you go to Bangalore, you might see many more options there than you see in Gurgaon. In Cyber City itself, there are so many women working, but I don't know if there are any crèches. We need professionally run, dependable facilities where you know that your child is within reach, is being taken care of, and you are still able to work. Somewhere that older kids can also go. I can promise that if I had that facility, I would not have quit or even taken on flexi-work as much as I did.

Five Things to Remember about This Dilemma

1. The workplace today has its share of pulls, pressures and stresses. A sabbatical will soon be a 'need to have' policy rather than a 'nice to have' policy. Taking a sabbatical is a personal choice and it helps if the organization is understanding.

2. There are many reasons for taking a sabbatical—to rejuvenate oneself, to take care of kids' education or growth, to take care of parents, to pursue a hobby, or to study. You must have a clear timeframe in your mind before you take the sabbatical.

3. Companies have different types of policies; some give an employee a paid sabbatical and some offer leave without pay. Whichever way it is, you need to be financially settled to take a sabbatical.

4. A typical sabbatical lasts at least six months. The first four to eight weeks are a period of unwinding, then comes a period of activity, and the last four weeks are

a period of preparing to get back to work. Use the time well.

5. It is important for organizations to change policies to enable more sabbaticals. This can be the next big policy for organizations to offer. CEOs and CHROs need to study the impact of sabbaticals in depth, and then tailor it to suit the individual. Sabbaticals work best when they are personalized for the employee.

Dilemma 6

Switching Industries in a Career

When an economy opens up, new industries and sectors emerge. In India, too, we have seen this occur, with telecom, airlines, retail, e-commerce and financial services opening up over the last two decades. And every new industry looks to the older ones in order to source talent. That's when a dilemma rears its head: *Should I stay in an industry I know, or make a switch to further my career?*

I have worked in FMCG and telecom, the construction industry and textiles. All are very different with new concepts to be learnt and practised, and yet they share some common principles that can be applied across the board. Joining a new industry is both exciting and challenging as you progress in your career.

According to a LinkedIn survey, one in three Indian professionals feel as if they are 'career sleepwalking—stagnant as though they are on a treadmill going nowhere'. More than half (57 per cent) say they would consider career pivoting. This is an important aspect when it comes to job-hopping, one that cannot be completely explained by the generational shift or the changed aspirations of millennials and Gen Z. Then what is it that fuels this lack of excitement? Sometimes, a boring industry.

Some industries are big and a number of companies come under their canopy, whereas some others comprise a smaller number of players. So, in an industry of significant size having many competitors, a manager can move around within it and still enjoy career progress. But in a small industry that houses only a few players, a very real need to change industries is felt, in order to grow in one's career.

Let's look at the FMCG sector. A \$65 billion industry, with about 1760 companies, wherein only 300 have a turnover of more than 10 crore rupees. But it promises plentiful scope for people to stay in the sector and make good progress in their career. It has ample capability, especially in distribution and branding, and other industries raid talent from the FMCG industry.

What Does the Trend-Line Tell Us?

1. Executives who are adaptable tend to do well when they switch industries, as this quality helps them learn the rules of the new industry and also understand the connections in the value chain.
2. Executives coming from large companies with established systems find it difficult to adjust to the culture and resources of a mid-size or small company. A large firm in one industry provides enormous comfort whereas getting used to a small or mid-sized firm in another industry takes time.

3. Every industry is going through a churn thanks to digitization and business model disruption. So, every industry is shedding jobs and some are hiring. This presents a people surplus on one hand but a skill-set deficiency on the other.

4. Employees feel that their learning curve has flattened and want to experience something new. So, they move from one industry to another. Large conglomerates that are home to multiple brands or categories can keep people engaged and enthused about the different options they can come up with. They have the wherewithal to offer good talent experiences across industries. For example, a talented manager in the Tata Group can move from the auto sector to software to FMCG, retail, steel and utilities. Such conglomerates have run a common cadre programme in the past but that doesn't seem so popular today.

5. Some companies are willing to hire outsiders while some others see the entry level as the starting point for new recruits and rely on in-house talent for all sectors. Globally, Procter & Gamble (P&G) is one such company; they rarely recruit at mid or senior levels. I have competed against P&G in hair care, fem care and baby care, directly. I have a lot of respect for them. When one of my colleagues, Niranjani, from the finance department of Nokia, told me that she had an offer with P&G, I wholeheartedly encouraged her to take it up because I strongly felt that her talent would bloom and thrive there. Today, she is CFO of Hershey India.

6. I have immense respect for ITC too. Years ago, they recognized that cigarettes would present a challenge, and so they set about pivoting to new streams of business, venturing into hotels, packaging, FMCG, paper, stationery, food, milk, etc. They went into each sector with home-grown managers and resisted the temptation to recruit from outside. This has worked well for ITC; their managers are usually adaptable and comfortable in new industries.

7. Internationally, you see both successful and unsuccessful examples of industry switching. Most media would label John Sculley's move from selling PepsiCo beverages to Apple technology a failure. Most media would rate Lou Gerstner's move from Amex and Nabisco to IBM a big success.

8. Here's a lesson for industry switchers at senior or CEO level. Typically, the media will start out sceptical and you will need to engage them and prove to them that you understand the value drivers of the new industry. You cannot win over every journalist, but you must try. Since you are new to the industry, the ecosystem will go by what the media prints. Hence, getting across the correct narrative is important.

9. We have seen executives from the private sector move into roles in government or public sector companies. Prakash Tandon, the first Indian chairman of Hindustan Lever, moved from Lever to STC (State Trading Corporation). He mentions in his book that the finance minister at the time sent him a telegram saying: 'Don't commit suicide.' We recently saw Nandan Nilekani do a

great job as Aadhaar chief, slipping into that role from his earlier position as CEO of Infosys. In a way, I see Debjani Ghosh, who moved from Intel to run NASSCOM, in a country and industry-building role. The most celebrated example is Robert McNamara, one of my early role models. McNamara was President of Ford Motor Company, before he went and worked for President Kennedy as secretary of defence, after which he became president of the World Bank. A rare example of a leader who proved successful across the spectrum of private enterprise, government, and a non-profit organization.

10. There are also many examples of spectacular failures among people who switch industries. This happens at senior levels when people come in as CEO from outside the industry. When I have analysed these failures, it comes down to poor adaptability and relying on outdated concepts that have worked in the past. The inability to play a new game with new rules is the problem. In such cases, the company and the media do a quiet burial and life moves on.

Where and When Does Industry Change Happen?

Here is a list of things you must think about as you consider a cross-industry move:

1. The definitions of a function matter when you look at industries. In most construction material and B2B (Business to Business) industries, the traditional customer-facing function is labelled Marketing. I would

urge you to understand the specific meaning of the function in each industry before you apply. Next comes Communications. In some industries, this encompasses both internal and external communications, whereas in some others, it refers to only external communications, essentially public relations. The other thing to check is the job title. I remember, in the beverages business of Hindustan Lever, there was a designation labelled territory sales manager, which was seen by the durable industry as a step above area sales manager, and we would constantly attract great CVs. In the case of beverages, a territory sales manager reported to an area sales manager. In short, please do your homework diligently when you look at making a cross-industry move.

2. Industry change happens regularly at the junior sales level and industries continually look to bringing in better execution capabilities. It starts with one junior manager moving from one company to another company in a new industry and spreading the word amongst his colleagues.

3. Capabilities in finance are fungible across industries; finance people are industry-agnostic.

4. Capabilities in R&D tend to be industry-constrained. Very few R&D professionals are able to move across industries, except those in basic areas which form a platform in the next industry.

5. Branding capabilities are pliable across industries. However, one has to keep in mind B2B companies versus B2C (Business to Consumer) companies. The concept of branding is different in these two industries. I have seen many technology companies hire people from allied

industries, such as advertising and communications, for branding roles.

6. HR managers transition smoothly and seamlessly across industries. I have seen many do well in different industries.

7. Supply chain managers are different for different industries. Industries looking to enhance their capability in this function tend to hire from leading edge industries where supply chain is critical. For example, supply chain is critical in the building construction material industry, where transportation costs and supply chain costs form a big chunk of total costs. I see a broad clustering of supply chain capabilities around technology, small packs and high volume, bulk product form, etc.

8. Go-to-market capabilities are industry-specific, and such talent will not move across industries easily.

9. Legal and government relations capabilities are industry-specific at one level, but the ecosystem one builds can be leveraged. I have seen many legal and government relations people do well by switching industries.

10. Finally, compensation varies in every industry, incentive plans are different, and the parameters of incentive change. So, please go through these variables in depth before making an assumption regarding the compensation. Words on the cost to company (CTC) sheet look different across industries.

Industry Hopping: How to Prepare?

You need to look at industries that are willing to accept outside talent. It is always good to do your homework and

Top 10 Industries Hiring Outside Their Industry (Global)

Industry	%
internet	11.8%
venture capital and private equity	11.1%
computer and network security	10.6%
online media	9.9%
staffing and recruiting	9.4%
computer software	8.8%
information services	8.3%
management consulting	8.2%
investment banking	8.2%
e-learning	8.2%

% of members joining industry from a different industry in 2014

speak to people in the new industry well before you accept the offer, or what's better, before you even consider making a switch.

Here is some data from India and the world

Are people moving industries simply out of boredom? HR experts say, familiarity with the industry causes boredom or disillusionment, which becomes a desire to move out from the sector. According to a Korn Ferry poll of nearly 5000 professionals in the US, the top reason people looked for a new job was because they needed a new challenge. A recent survey in the US says nearly half (49 per cent) of the respondents have made a dramatic career shift, say, from marketing to engineering, or teaching to finance. Globally, 34 per cent of users changed both function and company, as per LinkedIn's 2014 survey.

In India, about 45 per cent of the millennials showed likelihood of switching industries, compared to about 35 per cent Gen Zs, who are more likely to switch job functions while considering a career change. 'Overall, across generations, 44 per cent of respondents said they would consider changing companies versus 30 per cent respondents who would consider switching job functions (for example, marketing to product management),' adds LinkedIn. A survey by Executive Access shows that 65 per cent of CEOs are keen to switch industry compared to 30–35 per cent a few years ago. That's doubling in a few years. This is because, today, CEOs believe that their bigger impact comes from leadership skills, not hard or functional skills.

How prevalent are cross-functional switches in India? Devarajan says it's not that common yet, but organizations are willing to stretch and make things happen for high-potential resources sooner rather than later:

There are many more business roles or general managerial roles that are available at junior levels these days as compared to the past. Earlier, these were top of the pyramid roles. Today, small start-up ventures require cross-functional skills and capabilities. So, it has become more possible. But in large structured organizations, these moves are not that easily available. You have to move from one function to the other and it's not that easily done. People are also moving companies a lot more, rather than moving jobs within the company. That creates a problem because you want to test only one variable at a time; since you are already getting a resource from outside the company, you don't want to change the function at the same time. These are the realities of today. When it's possible, it's more at the instance of the individual.

Are Internal Function Moves Better Than Industry Change?

Wharton professors Matthew Bidwell and Ethan Mollick seem to agree with Devarajan. In a research paper, 'Shifts and Ladders: Comparing the Role of Internal and External Mobility in Executive Careers', they say: 'People who switch employers often land similar jobs as their old ones, because the new firm will be reluctant to place the new person in a job they have never done before.'

Employees, they add, receive the greatest, long-run benefits by taking different roles at their current company. 'It is those internal moves that lead to advances in pay, rank and responsibility, and provide long-term gains in pay and satisfaction,' Bidwell says. In contrast, switching employers leads to initial increases in pay but smaller career advancement benefits, usually with the same number of subordinates— managing the same number of people. Moreover, the number of times that workers moved across firms had little impact on how they were paid in the long run.

R.R. Nair professes slightly different views:

In the case of cross-sectoral exposures, in the past, people always felt that if you join FMCG or if you join an automotive company, you really step up and learn and grow. Therefore, your progress is assured in one sector. In today's fast-changing VUCA world, it becomes essential that you have multiple sectoral exposures and experiences because the business models are going to be different. There are unique technologies and unique customer-related features and challenges you are likely to experience in different sectors. Therefore, broad-basing one's experience around handling challenges in multiple sectors is critical. At least 3–4 sectoral exposures in a career spanning about 20–25 years is a good idea.

Of course, even long-term engagement with organizations and life-term employment itself is getting redefined. Careers such as mine, where you spent over thirty years in the same organization, are likely to be a rarity in the future. A lot of young people are also looking to either get into start-ups or breaking away from the traditional business context to taking up many voluntary endeavours in order to seek fulfilment and find their purpose in life by the time they are thirty-five.

We have seen how the workspace is getting reformed by younger professionals. Companies themselves are becoming less likely to nurture long-term career advancements within their ranks. 'The shift towards flatter organizational models also creates a greater need for internal mobility,' says Deloitte. But only 6 per cent of its respondents believed their organizations were excellent at enabling internal talent mobility. This reflects squarely in employees quitting or joining a company, citing lack of career progression—something that HR leaders need to note. Nair adds:

There are multiple ways by which one can get inter-functional exposure. I would advise anyone who is interested in moving into a general management role to definitely have multiple functional exposures. I would advocate that such a person, every three years in the early stage of their career, must look within the organization and express the desire to move into other functions, and therefore avail of job rotation opportunities. Come out of the comfort zone to do multiple jobs, so that you strengthen the breadth of your experience and exposure, besides being strong in one or two domains where more specialist and deeper interest lies.

To add to this, increasingly, even to do a domain-specialist role, by being part of cross-functional teams, your ability to collaborate with other functions is key; align your agenda with the overall agenda of the business and the function of the company gets accentuated. So, if one is aiming for senior levels and general management roles, there is no question that a person has to plan or seek opportunities for cross-functional roles.

The Right Move

But an industry change brings with it a plethora of questions and dilemmas. 'Impact on pay packets and designation hinders close to 51 per cent from making a career switch,' says LinkedIn. Acquiring new skills for a career change could need both time and money. Basing such a decision solely on money isn't right either. Often, people don't dig deep enough to see whether the sector is a good fit. The answer to why they want to change careers and what they want to get out of it is missing. Nair says:

> One has to actually look at what's the sort of career anchor the person seems to have. Here, I am referring to the work of Edgar Schein who has studied the careers of people, and conclude that people have about 8–9 different career anchors or career orientations. There are some people who want to be specialists and therefore want to stay in that specialist domain; there are some others who want to actually be in general management. So, depending upon the career anchor, the person has to choose whether to remain in the same function and grow in that function or to make an inter-functional move.

Besides this kind of introspection, reaching out to people in the target industry and company makes all the difference in making the correct decision as also in the subsequent learning that must happen. When you switch careers, it's your ability to learn new skills and pick up new habits that is vital. It means keeping the ego on the backburner, listening and learning from people who are probably younger than you. So too does drawing on the strengths and transferable skills you picked up in the previous career play a role.

> To be responsible for multiple functions calls for something more. You have to learn things which you have probably not done in your life at all. It's important

to have a network of people you could spend time with, seek clarifications and get insight into the nuances of the function that you are new to. It's also important to make a collaborative commitment to making the team succeed. Often, youngsters in the organization believe that they have to prove themselves to grow. I think that the willingness to be team-oriented is important when you move across functions.

In a general managerial position, quite often, it is required that you get a specialist to add value, contribute and build the perspective and concept. The willingness to have your thought process challenged and value added by others is important. Be willing to take risks because, when you are operating in areas that you have not worked in before, you have to try, you have to experiment.

All said and done, despite the challenges, even late-life career changes often result in a positive emotional outlook, according to a study. 'The New Careers for Older Workers' study, conducted by AIER, found that 82 per cent of the survey participants who made a career change after the age of forty-five were successful in their transition. What's more, these individuals reported that they were happier in their new positions, with many earning more after the switch than they did earlier.

My Personal Lessons

I spoke with at least 200 people before I moved to telecom and Nokia. Each conversation helped me understand the opportunities and challenges that lay ahead. I also got to know the key players in the new industry through these conversations.

Manoj Kohli in Airtel and Sandip Das in Vodafone helped organize industry induction sessions after I joined.

When I went back to FMCG and joined PepsiCo, I talked to about 100 people about the industry. After I joined, I went and spent time with some of the stalwarts of the industry—Vinita Bali, ex-Coca-Cola; Vibha Rishi Paul, ex-PepsiCo; and Ramesh Chauhan, the leading light of the beverages industry; as well as my predecessors on the job.

In other words, there is no substitute to preparation when one switches industries.

Piyush Pandey, chief creative officer, worldwide, and executive chairman, India, O&M

Piyush Pandey is one of the most recognizable names in Indian advertising. He began his career as a professional cricketer. He also worked as a tea taster for Goodricke Group before joining Ogilvy & Mather in Mumbai in 1979. He's been a career O&M man ever since, rising up the ranks to head the organization globally, from India.

You've been a one-company man all your life. What made you stay with O&M all along?

I joined O&M and, within months, I got a job offer from Vazir Sultan Tobacco. They were going to look after me much better, allow me to play cricket, post me in Jaipur, give me a home and a car. But by that time, I had tasted advertising, and I was enjoying it. The main driving force in my life has been to do what I really enjoy doing. Therefore, I refused that offer and stuck around in Mumbai, travelling in third-class compartments.

Why do people have a dilemma? People have dilemmas when they are chasing money, when they are chasing designations, when their name is not on the board, etc. I had no such dilemmas. I was enjoying my work, getting the kind of money that I was happy with, and the people and clients were wonderful. I was just having a really good time. It has been thirty-eight years now. Over the years, I have changed jobs within the organization—I joined client servicing, I was asked to run the office also, and then I became national creative director. Then I was asked to run the company. But I never left what was my forte, which was creative. So, I had no reason whatsoever to leave.

Debjani Ghosh, president, NASSCOM

Debjani Ghosh is currently the president of NASSCOM. In 2018, she was felicitated by the President of India at the 'First Ladies' programme, which honours exceptional women pioneers. Her name is on the '100 Most Influential Women in UK–India Relations: Celebrating Women' list. She was named the 'Tech Leader of the Year 2020' by Vogue *and was listed among 'India's most powerful women in tech' by* Business Today. *She was also the first woman to lead Intel India and MAIT.*

You have worked in technology right through your career. What are the advantages of staying in one industry and what are the disadvantages? Did you ever think of moving industry?

For me, technology is a passion. So, having the opportunity to work with something I strongly believe in has been an amazing blessing. Also, I don't see tech as a vertical. It's a horizontal layer that runs across all verticals from manufacturing to services to products, etc., providing them with the tools and ability to drive the transformations needed for success. Hence, the opportunity to learn is endless. In fact, I have worked in multiple roles despite staying in the same field. It has never felt like status quo, and whenever I start feeling comfortable in a role, I know it's time for me move on to something new that will give me the ability to challenge myself further.

You moved from running Intel to running NASSCOM as its president. This must have been a tough decision to make. What factors played out in this dilemma, who helped you make the decision before you made it, and how did people react to the move? How did you handle the naysayers?

It was actually one of the easiest decisions to make. I love technology for what it does—the impact it has on our lives. And when you apply the people lens to technology, India is a dream playground because of the huge challenges that technology can solve in this country. Since returning to India, that had been my obsession, and after a point I was clear that I needed to find a platform that would enable me to do much more to drive impact. NASSCOM was the dream platform. It offered me the opportunity to work with government and industry to shape the India Tech playbook. There were no second thoughts about whether I should do it or not. This was something I badly wanted. There weren't any naysayers. Every single one of my mentors felt that it was the best platform possible for me, given how passionate I was about technology and India. And the support I have got from the industry and the government is just overwhelming.

You are the first woman president of NASSCOM and definitely not the last. What changed for you when you took up the role, what advantages did you see and what challenges did you encounter?

Gender has never been a thing for me and it never will be. I don't want be known as the first woman president of NASSCOM but the best one. I am lucky to head this position at a time when the industry has to reinvent itself. I believe NASSCOM will play a critical role in shaping the new playbook and narrative. The building blocks I believe need to form the foundation of our industry are Trust, Talent, People-led Innovation, Inclusion and Agility. If we can build our competitive advantage along these lines, we would lead the world with focus on impact. My dream is that when the world thinks digital, the world will think India. The work I do to enable that will be my legacy, not my gender.

(Late) Chandramouli Venkatesan, former CEO (special projects), Pidilite Industries

Chandramouli Venkatesan was a corporate veteran with over twenty-six years of experience in the industry. He is also a bestselling author of two books—Get Better at Getting Better and Catalyst, *which earned rave reviews and made him a regular on the speaking circuit. After graduating from XLRI Jamshedpur, he started his career with Asian Paints, then moved to Onida. Before assuming his Pidilite corporate role, he served as managing director for Mondelēz India (erstwhile Cadbury India), where he did stints for over eleven years in a variety of roles spanning marketing, HR and business leadership, at India and Asia Pacific levels.*

You are essentially a sales and marketing professional, who also did a stint as HR head in Mondelēz. What made you switch roles?

It was circumstantial. They wanted a business development person to take up the HR head's role. So, they spoke to me to see if I would be interested. My manager wanted me to do it. Left to me, I might not have even initiated that conversation.

What were the skills that stood you in good stead to switch successfully?

When you make these cross-functional moves at a very senior level, the primary skill is leadership and organization management. That is quite transferable. I also had a lot of grounding in marketing and found that a lot of marketing skills are transferable. Fundamentally, in my own mind, I replaced a consumer with an employee. Now, your product is the company and the people who are employed with you. You want them to stay employed with you and not leave. At the same time, you have to attract new people from outside to be your employees. So, I did find that the core structure of a lot of marketing skills, such as segmentation, positioning, designing an offer, etc., were quite useful while working in HR as well.

Weren't you scared that this move might be seen as a demotion in some circles?

Sometimes it can be seen like that because there is a natural hierarchy to functions. So, when you move from marketing to HR, people might think that this person is demoted. But, personally, I had confidence in my reputation. I had a great relationship with my boss and colleagues. More importantly, he said that if I didn't like it, after a period, he would make sure I found a job back in the business. That commitment was important. Otherwise, there could have been hesitation in making this decision.

What advice will you give to young managers who are given a job rotation outside their core area? How should they prepare themselves?

Job rotation is not a fancy thing that everybody must do. There are many people who have suffered. None of these things should become formulaic. Careers are a lot more about using every opportunity that comes your way than using formulae. But if you do want to do job rotation, be clear on why you are doing it. There are two purposes you could have. One is that you don't necessarily enjoy what you are doing right now and want to find a new domain or a new function. The second is wanting to learn or develop yourself as a leader. So, it is important to be clear on the why of job rotation. A lot of people do it without any clarity on the why. Don't do it just because it's the trend.

Assuming that one is doing it for the right reasons, when is it best to do a job rotation outside your function—at junior level, mid-level or senior level?

I don't think there is a formula to it. But if you want to change your domain forever and no longer want to be in finance and want to be in sales, then the earlier in life you move, the better. Alternatively, if you want to just draw functional experience, then you must build a strong foundation somewhere, master something and make a move.

When you do make such moves, should you be looking for some guarantees from the company or the boss who is hiring you in a new vertical, because you are not coming there on an equal footing?

Honestly, this is a very complex thing, so I won't give advice on whether or not you should look for guarantees.

These things are very circumstantial. Sometimes, if you are coming with a mindset that, if it doesn't work for me, I will go back, then you are not going to work hard enough to make it work. Sometimes, having an exit option can make one a little casual. One needs do these things with a correct mindset.

Kirthiga Reddy, partner, SoftBank Investment Advisers, and former managing director, Facebook India and South Asia

You were heading the R&D centre of Facebook in Hyderabad and then moved as Facebook's first India CEO. How did you make that shift? Was it easy or difficult to move functions, and what new capabilities did you need to build?

I was employee #1 and managing director of Facebook India and South Asia. The first task was to build Facebook's operations centre in India. It was Facebook's fourth centre. Together, these global centres serve over three billion people today who use Facebook's services. When I joined, trusted advisers asked, 'Why move from a product role to an operations role? People usually want to move from operations to product.' My answer: 'This is Facebook. I believe in the mission, vision and the people. I would do any role for this company!'

In terms of shifting functions, the best piece of advice I received was from Sheryl Sandberg, COO Facebook. She told me, 'Kirthiga, you haven't risen through the ranks in the operations organization. Learn the nitty-gritty of what individual contributors do. That's the foundation to operate effectively at a 20,000-foot level.' At Facebook, I would shadow different parts of the operations organization every week to learn and to keep pace with the evolution. I have taken this to heart in each of my role changes as I learnt about new functions, new industries and new cultures—to name a few of the new capabilities I needed to build.

You moved from Facebook to SoftBank Investment Advisers. Again, what shifts in capabilities were needed here, and how did you manage it?

I joined SoftBank Investment Advisers (SBIA), manager of the $100B+ SoftBank Vision Fund, as their first female investment partner. My focus is Frontier, Enterprise and Health Tech.

My career leading up to my current role was about leading technology transformations—high-performance computing with SGI, the mobile shift with Good Technology, and the social shift with Facebook. As Deep Nishar, senior managing partner, SBIA, highlighted when I was considering the SBIA opportunity, my current role allows me the opportunity to be 'part of several technology transformations at the same time' and see the impact on people, communities and economies.

In terms of shifts in capabilities and how I managed it, it was a two-fold process. One was leveraging my strengths, like the know-how of what it takes to scale global businesses, having led multi-$100M businesses. The other was to go deep into all that I needed to learn—new industry, new investment sectors, new culture. I am grateful for my time at Stanford Business School that has given me a deep love of learning, the advice from Sheryl to understand the nitty-gritty of the role and the support from Deep and my colleagues who deeply invested in me.

Rohit Kale, MD, Spencer Stuart India

Rohit holds an MBA from IIM Calcutta. He began his career as a project engineer with Thermax Limited, helping erect and commission utility boilers. He currently leads Spencer Stuart's business in India and is a member of the consumer, energy and business and professional services practices. He has more than fifteen years of wide-ranging industry experience in consulting, banking and HR with organizations around the world. Before joining Spencer Stuart, Rohit was associate principal with McKinsey & Company in Mumbai and London, prior to which he spent six years with HSBC in their consumer banking division in Mumbai and Hong Kong.

You made a move from McKinsey to Spencer Stuart. What prompted this cross-functional change, and what variables did you consider while doing it?

I have actually had three journeys. I was working with HSBC in India and then Hong Kong, moved from there to McKinsey, and from there to Spencer Stuart. There were different reasons for making these moves. The HSBC to McKinsey move was straightforward. I was doing credit risk, and one of the things I was working on was credit card profitability. There, essentially, you push the customer to the edge, but don't let that customer fall over. If the customer falls over, you are not profitable. If the customer is not on the edge and is very comfortable, then you are not making any money. So, fundamentally, as a bank, you make money only when you get your customer to the edge. And you are constantly figuring out ways to push that customer to get to the edge. That didn't gel with my value system.

McKinsey was and remains one of our pre-eminent firms and the job there happened by chance. I wasn't looking for anything at that point. But it just seemed right and went on for quite some time. But I couldn't deal with the Monday-to-Friday travel. I was at a point where my dilemma was how to strike a balance between my personal and professional life. Professionally, McKinsey was the most fulfilling role I did, and in that context, the decision to leave was very difficult. But personally, it was very taxing. My daughter was two years old; my wife has a difficult career—

she is a doctor, so she is also not there on Saturdays. We weren't spending time together. I used to literally calculate what flight to take so that I could get two more hours with my daughter. And it was my EA who pointed this out to me, questioning what kind of life it was where I was counting the number of hours I would get to spend with my daughter every week.

That's when the penny dropped. While leaving was a difficult decision to make, I had to think about other options. And that was the challenge. Every other option in comparison looked meh. So, I had to find something that fit in with my values. That's when I came to Spencer Stuart asking for career advice. What I realized was that everything else put together, this was a fit. And the moment I saw that, it caught my interest because, fundamentally, it was still about solving clients' problems. At McKinsey, I was solving business problems; here, I would be solving people problems. But the context of what I was doing wouldn't change.

One of the things that I learnt in this whole process was to ask the important question—*What are the things that drive you*? It is important to understand that. Is it the content of what you do? The people you work with? The position of authority? The lifestyle, the glamour? Hobnobbing with the rich and the famous? I realized that trying to understand what drives you is vital, and not many people actually do it. Even when I have these discussions with professionals and ask them this question, it is very poorly articulated, or people haven't really spent time really questioning it. Everybody has a set of drivers, but what are the most important ones?

What practice were you handling at McKinsey and how difficult was it to make the change to headhunting?

I did everything except financial services—a lot of industrial, consumer and infrastructure-related work. Now, I do primary consumer and retail. So, in many ways, the content of what I do, I have realized, doesn't matter. Subject matter is not something that drives me.

McKinsey gives you a certain calling card. To give up on that calling card that was, in some ways, your identity was tough. The move forced me to develop my own identity as an individual. I learnt a lot about myself on that journey. For example, one of the things I enjoyed at McKinsey was client service. I liked having an impact. I liked the fact that I didn't really have a boss looking over my shoulder all the time. I liked the fact that I was in control of my own schedule. And I could decide what I wanted to do, and how and when I wanted to do it. I understood all this to some extent and realized that a classical corporate job was not for me. I realized I was never going to be able to be a corporate person again. That's not the job I want.

The other thing at the time was the whole start-up boom. Many of my friends were convincing me to join them. And some of them have become billionaires. McKinsey, in particular, has spawned a very large number of successful start-ups. I had an opportunity to be part of that journey, and, again, the big decision was whether or not to do it. Because that start-up journey essentially meant working weekends and 14–15 hours a day. I had done that in the past. I was at a stage where I didn't want to do that. I may not have gotten that massive value creation opportunity, but I was okay with that.

Since you've straddled so many industries and functions, are there any threads that run common to all?

Strictly speaking, problem solving is problem solving. What people care about is the same thing. Fundamentally, P&L is P&L, irrespective of what sector you are in. So, understanding what the drivers of P&L or business are is the most important thing that I have picked up across industries.

Wearing your headhunter hat, when you put candidates into cross-industry roles, what are the some of the attributes that you look for in them?

I do look at the background of the individual. One of the things that you are looking for is strong IQ. Because if you are looking at a new industry, you have to pick up the nuances of the industry quickly. And one proxy for that is, at least in the Indian context, which colleges did you go to and how well did you do in college. It's not a perfect measure, but it is one of the proxies that we use to try and figure things out. The other thing is resilience. And again, the context of education helps you, because, if you have slogged your way into an IIT or an IIM, then we know that you are a fighter. Another thing we look for is culture adaptability. Has the candidate really adapted to a different culture? Or has the person been primarily in one company or one type of company all his life? Have they gone on to do something intrapreneurial? Set up a new business? What has the person shown in terms of building something versus applying a template? Can the person set something up from scratch or do they only adapt? All of this matters, because, when you are coming into a new industry, you are going to have to very quickly pick up on issues and execute. And, most importantly, there is no formula. We have to set up the formula.

How amenable are clients or the industry in general to hiring people from outside?

Everyone is open on the face of it. But when it comes to selecting two people and making the final decision, it comes down to who knows the business. Unfortunately, a lot of the clients still go with experience versus potential. Between someone with relevant experience and higher potential, relevant experience still gets more weightage. The other mistake that many clients make is that they almost ignore the culture fit.

At what stage of the industry are people open to picking up candidates from outside? Is it easier at a higher level where it's more to do with leadership and strategy and less with subject matter expertise?

I will give you a classic example. If you need somebody as head of sales in an FMCG company, it is tough to find a generalist. There are strong functional roles where it is difficult to convince clients to take on a generalist. For business roles, it is easier. But the challenge is how do you get a generalist to fit into a business role? That's a big risk. OYO is a massive believer in generalists.

So, if they want a head of supply, they will want someone who's done management consulting. Aditya Ghosh is the only person they've hired with somewhat relevant experience in that sector. Their head of Middle East and South East Asia is a management consultant from McKinsey who is a qualified doctor—a proper medical doctor, and he was part of the healthcare practice at McKinsey. They have generalists almost everywhere, and of course, it is a bit forced by the fact that they don't have an industry to hire from. It has served them extremely well.

What should people looking to move industries learn? Any new capabilities or skills that they must acquire?

Humility. Because you have to be ready to accept the fact that you don't know anything and therefore have to learn from one down. You will have to learn from the entire ecosystem and not come in with the 'I am CEO' or 'I am the leader, therefore I am supposed to know everything' attitude. It is okay for you not to know everything. But humility is a very difficult thing to learn. It is either there or not there.

Do candidates develop industry myopia if they stay in one industry for long?

Yes, and it is not a good thing. Because a glass ceiling develops for people who have done that. There are some lucky ones who are able to have a long career in just one industry, but for many who don't rise to the very top, they find themselves too old to do the same job and too irrelevant beyond the sector. They know their sector, so they become advisors or consultants. But their career peters out. So, it is always good to make one or two moves because it enables you to have a life beyond sixty.

Sonny Iqbal, co-head, Egon Zehnder

Sonny earned a BA with honours from St Stephen's College, Delhi University, followed by an MBA from the University of Surrey, UK, and a postgraduate diploma in hospitality from the Oberoi Centre for Learning and Development, Delhi. Prior to joining Egon Zehnder, he worked for the Oberoi Group in the UK, India and the Middle East in operations and marketing roles, and also managed the financial and travel services business of American Express in India. He then helped found Egon Zehnder's offices in New Delhi, Bangalore and Mumbai, and is currently active in the company's health, consumer, board, and executive assessment and development practices. He is also co-leader of the global family business advisory practice and advises businesses on succession, founder transition, governance and family charter development across multiple continents and markets.

You made a cross-industry move from hospitality to credit cards to leadership advisory. How difficult was it for you?

All the work that I have done has had a lot to do with people, whether it's professional services or hospitality, travel or credit cards. So, it's always been about the joy of working with people and handling different situations, and less about being driven by industries.

I think where industry considerations come in is where subject matter and content become a huge driver. That's where there needs to be a right balance between one's motivation and one's subject matter. How I've been fortunate is that when I made all these moves, the industries in India were nascent, so we could easily shift across them.

When you made a cross-industry move, what enabled you to settle down there in terms of understanding the subject

matter, or other intricacies? In your opinion, how should one settle down when making cross-industry moves?

These things are often governed by factors that are not very easy to recognize but are actually discernible in the lives of people who have evolved and grown. These factors aren't hard, they aren't quantifiable; rather, they are concerned with motivation, your ability to learn, how curious you are in adapting to a new environment, in asking the right questions and recognizing the softer signals. To a large degree, it has also got to do with the nature of engagement that an individual has, with how they engage with people. Engagement can mean how you handle your vulnerability when you do not know something, and the environment letting you come to terms with that vulnerability without judging you. Those who succeed in these transitions usually manage these things well. They are driven by inherent traits, such as the manner in which they engage, their curiosity, and determination that allows them to work through difficult situations. It is less driven by subject matter, unless you are in a very high subject-matter driven industry. So, for instance, if you are a scientist, you have to be a very good scientist.

Are there core capabilities or transferable skills that apply to every industry? If so, what are they?

The idea of skills being transferable does not fit well in my mind because I believe one develops them over time by doing a job well. If you have grown up working in the auto industry and you become a good salesman, but you have forgotten how to evolve along other dimensions, then it is a problem. So skills alone are insufficient.

In what circumstances do employees typically look for or want people from outside the industry?

There are some industries in which, at a particular point in a person's career, the skills count and then after a particular period of time, many other things count. Some of those things I mentioned earlier. Intellect and leadership ability make up a very strong component. But a lot of it also has to do with people's inherent drivers. It is your desire to learn and grow that rouses the required motivation to keep expanding your horizons. Good leadership has multiple facets to it, including showing vulnerability and learning about yourself from a variety of sources that bring growth. At senior levels, skills and subject matter are not irrelevant; rather, a lot of other factors become more relevant.

Are there circumstances in which you would recommend not switching to another industry?

It depends on what stage of life you are in. Also, if the requirement to know your subject matter is inordinately high and you don't know too much about it, the move would be a little risky. When you make a move, it's not just about you; it's also about how others see you and how you are accepted as a leader. The more important point is, very often, when thinking about cross-industry change, people only think about where they want to go. They don't look at themselves from others' perspectives and ask if they are relevant for or good at what they want to do. A fair amount of thought needs to be given to that.

Sudhanshu Vats, former CEO, Viacom 18 Media, and CEO, Essel Propack

Post your second stint at HUL, you made a complete pivot again and decided to join the entertainment industry. What made you do that?

What happened around 2011–12 was that I had reached a level within Unilever which is internally called 4B. If you look at Unilever's work levels, they start with Level 1 and go up to Level 6. I was doing very well, and at 4B, I had the potential to get to Level 5, which was made up of only about ninety managers across the world. Similarly, 4B comprised only about 200. In India, however there was only a single role at Level 5, that of the CEO. And this role was at least 4–5 years away. There was a 20 to 25 per cent chance of getting it. I was among the four or five people who could have landed the job.

The other option was to step out of India. But my wife had a career here, and at that point, she was knocking at a partnership with PwC. So, from a family point of view, it was tough. Our elder daughter was entering Class 9, and we were very keen that she attended high school in India. So, while Unilever would have offered great opportunities outside, in different parts of the world, we were not ready as a family to step out of India at that point of time. That sparked a desire to be open to other things. Also, I was clear that I would move on as a CEO, but I was not hung up on any particular sector. I wanted to be CEO of a mid-size organization because, realistically, nobody would have given me that role in a large-size organization.

Being sector-agnostic has really served you well. Does it come naturally to you to want to enter uncharted territories and try new things?

Yes. I was always willing to jump. I think I am a good listener and a keen learner. I am a trekker at heart and a marathon runner. But when you do running and trekking, what happens is that you climb one peak, then you say, let's try the next one. So, I've always thought like this—*Okay, this is done, now what do I do next*?

You've balanced three different worlds—FMCG, lubricants, entertainment. How difficult is it to learn the ropes of a new industry or a new sector? And how did you go about doing it?

I think some people like to make changes, while others are not as comfortable jumping or taking risks. I found it quite easy. So, I'll answer this from my perspective. If you are secure as a person, I think that really helps. Second, you have to have an open mind. Third is curiosity and the desire to learn. And fourth, the humility and ability to listen. I think if you have these 3–4 ingredients, you can see that there are a lot of other things that are actually common between industries. There are certain things that are different, but you have to retain what is common. And you have to imbibe and learn things that are different when you begin a new chapter. You must carry the learnings forward, but not necessarily the mould. There is a difference between the mould and the learning. Learning can be shaped and contextualized. Moulds can be very hard-wired, though. And if you try and fit a mould, it becomes what you call a 'square peg in a round hole' kind of challenge.

Elaborate on the particular difficulties or challenges that you faced while shifting industries and how you overcame them.

Let me give you an example. I moved from Unilever, an FMCG giant, to Viacom 18, a media company. These are two different worlds. Unilever was far more data-driven. There was so much more research. You made a lot of informed decisions based on data. And the pace of change, compared to that in media, was a little lower, slower. Quality of talent was much higher as also less diverse. So, it was cast in a particular mould—chemical engineers, top IIT and IIM graduates—all fantastic minds. But when I moved to the media, the challenge was—you don't have that much data, and you're supposed to make calls which are not necessarily always fully informed by data. There is a lot of intuition involved. You have to mix intuition with data. It moves at a very rapid pace. Then you look at talent. I did not have that classical Unilever talent. But I realized that these youngsters are very passionate. And they have a slightly different balance between left brain and right brain, yet, basically, they bring a lot of passion into what they do.

That was a key learning for me, actually. That you have to be open and you have to rewire. And as long as you're open, it helps. This is something I've done since childhood. Start with a whiteboard. Don't get too carried away. Even at Unilever, where there would be dossiers on everyone, and dossiers are very useful, I would form a first impression of the person by starting on a clean slate or a whiteboard.

But how do people view you when you come from outside the industry? What are some markers to judge if they are accepting you?

When I moved here, there were a lot of people in my team, many with either phenomenal experience in general, or particularly in media. Many of them thought, *What is this guy from outside going to do here*? Therefore, initially, people are always watching, and for want of a better word, maybe even judging you. They see what moves are you making, how you are going forward. There are different styles, but I will tell you about the one I follow. I want to take them along and bring out the best in them, and I want to treat them with respect and dignity. That way, half the battle is won. I wouldn't say it is always won only by this method, but I do believe half the battle is won.

The person may still wonder, *'Why the hell is he here?'* But over a period of time, you start winning them over, bit by bit. The other thing I've always followed in all my big switches is that I first listen and then absorb, and I try to build on what is there. I am never in a tearing hurry to first demolish or bring down what was built, and then build again. There are different philosophies. For me, trying to build on what was there has always worked because it makes the other side more comfortable. They see that you are not overtly critical of everything they have done. And sometimes, as leaders and managers, we have a tendency to be to be in a hurry, to be very critical of the work done before us in the past. But many times, we don't have the context of all the decisions that are taken at a point in time. My ongoing hypothesis is that everyone tries to do the best they can at any point in time. And if you go with that theory, it helps, because then you are not overly critical.

What were some of the learnings you brought in from a previous job that you sort of put into place in a new

industry, and what were some of the things you had to completely unlearn in order to adjust to a new industry?

The first thing that I brought with me in abundance from Unilever to Viacom 18 was an understanding of the Indian consumer and a bit of a first-hand feel of storytelling as a marketing professional who had done over hundred advertisements in his tenure. The second area where there were applicable learnings was to do with how distribution worked in FMCG. That was somewhat comparable. So, an understanding of the market landscape and the distribution landscape is helpful in any other industry.

I think the difference was to bring together in one room a very diverse set of people from very different backgrounds and ways of thinking, and sometimes, slightly different motivations as well. To be able to come together and create something from that is what happens in the media. Whereas, in FMCG, it was a more homogeneous set of people with the same set of educational skills, and a somewhat similar style of thinking and working. This was more creative, and the question we worked on was taking an idea, then looking at how the idea can be blown up without necessarily being fully backed by data.

When I came in, I listened for about six months, and I talked to people. Then we put together a five-year plan. I remember when I was first putting together a five-year plan, most people were sceptical about what a five-year

> plan would do. But we co-created values. The five values we live with are: 'Create Tomorrow, Stay Bold, Stay Curious, Listen Deeply, Learn with Humility and Execute with Excellence.'

Five Things to Remember about This Dilemma

1. New industries come up as an economy opens up and grows. New industries have a technology impact on traditional industries. These new industries need tried-and-tested talent from some marquee industries to run their business. We will see more opportunities for cross-industry movement in the future.

2. Be clear about why you are picking the new industry and do your homework. Talk to people in that industry and see how your capabilities will shine there. Would the move to this industry leverage any of your current strengths and would it also give you new capabilities?

3. There is no substitute to preparation when you consider moving to a new industry. Get as much knowledge as possible about the industry, its ecosystem, its people. Today, you will find many analysts' reports on every possible industry available on the Internet.

4. Some capabilities and functions are industry-tied while others can move across industries. You have to be sure of your function and its applicability across industries.

5. Large companies can offer you challenging roles within the same company. Conglomerates can offer you different

industry experience under the same umbrella. If you are working in a large company or a conglomerate, think deeply before moving out. It's better to be clear that the company cannot take care of your interests before you switch industries.

Dilemma 7

Should I Take up an Overseas Job?

In the 1990s, working overseas was a must-have item on a CV. That charm is still there, but it doesn't have the same value as before. Is going overseas good for my CV? Would it help me accelerate my career? Would it help me build assets? Should I stay overseas or come back? Would there be good jobs for me if I choose to come back to India? These are the questions associated with this dilemma.

Working overseas in the past was a no-brainer. It provided more money as the Indian rupee kept depreciating; it gave the manager access to the MNC headquarters if he/she were posted there; it also told the manager that he was a valued resource and was therefore being groomed for something better. There were two types of moves in multinational organizations—one, a one-way ticket where the home country shouldered no further responsibility for your career once you left its shores, and the other a commitment to bring the manager back to the home country.

In the last twenty years, most multinationals have established regional offices to break the span of control from the centre. In the past, the regional offices were also housed in the head office as another department. Popular regional hubs include Dubai, Singapore, Hong Kong, Geneva, London, Johannesburg and Nairobi. MNCs decided the regional location based on your sales mix and the tax benefits of setting up a regional office.

Let's look at the data and understand the way this working abroad concept has evolved.

1. Indians are the word's talent bank. The United Nations (UN) estimated India as the leading country of origin of international migrants in 2019, with a 17.5 million-strong diaspora. This number was seven million in 1990. This constitutes all types of jobs, from agricultural labour going to Australia and New Zealand to employment in the Middle East. Africa has been a destination for many white-collar jobs, with firms having established a base in Africa in the last ten years. India also receives more remittances from migrants than any other country. There is a plus side to all this. India got $79 billion from remittances of the Indian diaspora in 2018, according to the World Bank.

2. Globally, the number of people wanting to work in another country has dropped. The overall willingness to emigrate has dipped—57 per cent of respondents in a 2018 BCG survey say they would move to another country for work as opposed to 64 per cent in 2014. Tightening trade and immigration policies have had an

impact here. 'The changes brought about by heightened nationalism show up in the survey results—sometimes subtly, sometimes less so,' says BCG.

3. India also sees a drop in the willingness to go abroad. The preference for foreign work locations has seen a 10 per cent drop amongst Indians to 60 per cent in a 2018 Times Jobs survey. There are reports of Indians coming back home as better opportunities, especially at the senior levels, open up in sectors such as IT, healthcare and pharma among others. 'Many multinationals are moving toward the creation of a strong Indian business unit and, in the process, moving away from functions or global products as the primary axis of governance,' explains McKinsey.

4. The Indian subsidiaries of most multinational companies have done well and are in the Top 10 countrywide list for revenue and profitability. This seat at the high table for India has given many talented managers an opportunity to shine in good roles outside the country as well. Indians want to work for an MNC. The Randstad 2019 survey showed that 55 per cent of Indians preferred to work for a large multinational corporation, while only 9 per cent preferred start-ups. The preference for MNCs is strongly attributed to job security, financial health and career-progression opportunities that MNCs are able to offer their employees. However, I personally believe that things are changing with the constant restructuring that MNCs go through. This makes people in an MNC live in perpetual anxiety from year to year, which is why many of their executives are choosing a more secure environment.

5. Migration is good for the global economy. This debate around global migration has real economic benefits too. 'Workers moving to higher-productivity settings boosts global GDP. MGI estimates that migrants contributed roughly 6.7 trillion, or 9.4 per cent, to global GDP in 2015—some $3 trillion more than they would have produced in their origin countries,' says McKinsey.

6. Where do Indians love to go? Here is a pie chart depicting today's favoured destinations:

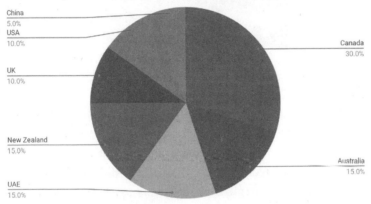

Favoured Spot for Indians Looking for Overseas Employment

China 5.0%
USA 10.0%
UK 10.0%
New Zealand 15.0%
UAE 15.0%
Canada 30.0%
Australia 15.0%

7. If you see the above pie chart, three countries—New Zealand, Canada and Australia—are high on work-life balance. Even the reasons why people want to live abroad have undergone a change, according to BCG. In 2014, the top reason was to broaden one's personal experience. 'Personal experience still matters in 2018, but two more practical motivations—better career opportunities and a better standard of living—have risen in importance.'

Career development is the top consideration in three of the biggest emerging economies: China, India and Brazil.

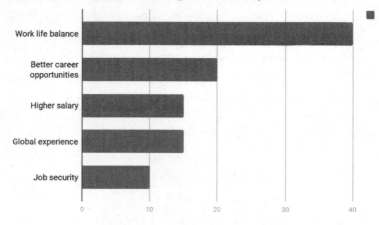

Top reasons Indians are looking for overseas jobs

8. HSBC Expat's survey shows that, of all overseas workers, millennials and Gen Z employees enjoyed the greatest step up in terms of earnings and career progression. The average eighteen- to thirty-four-year-old's earnings rose 35 per cent after relocating overseas. Not surprisingly, this is the group most enthused to explore overseas shores, and also the most coveted among employers. 'It's younger employees—with their malleability, up-to-the-minute technical know-how, ambition and stamina—that foreign countries and multinational companies want to hire in the first place,' says BCG. Like elsewhere, it's the juniors who are eager to work abroad (70 per cent), followed by middle-level employees (50 per cent) and seniors (40 per cent) from India.

9. The triumvirate of skill expansion, networking and money—all play a part in making overseas jobs lucrative. Increasingly, work-life balance is significant too, second to monetary considerations for US employees; 64 per cent in the Randstad survey say they would move just for a better work-life balance. It also tops the chart for Indians looking for overseas jobs.

10. We see a trend where global companies are setting up centres of excellence in India. MNCs are setting up research hubs, there is work being done in the areas of big data, analytics, AI—a far cry from the early days of outsourcing back-office functions. The salaries on offer are competitive, promising a lifestyle that's better value for the money than it is abroad. Importantly, it's a way out of the uncertainty for Indian nationals, who, along with other migrants, are facing a stricter visa regime and even mistrust and anger from the locals.

So how does one work through this dilemma?

a. Language plays an important role as your first decision point. Indians are fluent in English and they think in English ahead of their mother tongue in most white-collar roles. Getting a role in an English-speaking country would help. Having to learn the language becomes so much more of a challenge. My predecessor in Hindustan Lever, Prakash Nedungadi, got a break in Germany and he diligently learnt German for six months before moving there.

b. Is this a one-way ticket or is there a return ticket—this should be your next consideration. When I moved to run emerging markets in Nokia from Dubai, I knew that there was no role for me back in India. So, I had to plan everything on the basis of Dubai or Finland. This has a big bearing on your family and whether you will uproot them.

c. Even if a multinational is sending you to another subsidiary, please check all the conditions in that subsidiary. Unilever posted a few people from India to Egypt, at a subsidiary run by a local entrepreneur. He ran the company as his own and people who didn't meet his list came back disappointed. Unilever could do little to help.

d. If a multinational sends you to another country, the business model could be different. In the global beverages business, both Coca-Cola and PepsiCo use large bottlers; so while you might be posted to Saudi Arabia or Philippines, in effect, you manage the bottler relationship and his organization runs the daily execution. Does the job present the right challenge in these situations—this is something you must consider.

e. If you go to the Middle East, the visa is given to the company, and it is not easy for you to switch companies. If a company has no role for you, then your visa stands cancelled and you need to go back.

f. It could well happen that good roles are not available to you once you move out of India. This is a discussion you will need to have with the company, stating your preferred roles and the options they may have—that is, your willingness to come back if the role opens up.

g. Here is one thing I have seen personally at close quarters. If you go abroad, please do keep in touch with headhunters and a few senior leaders. I have heard many middle-level and senior managers say that head hunters seem to forget them once they are not in India. You must build your own network if you want to come back and not rely on the company network.

h. I think after the COVID-19 pandemic and work from home (WFH), I see fewer jobs available globally. Most companies would want you to work from home even if you are doing a global or regional role. This concept of location-free roles will catch on.

i. Even if you want to go abroad for work, try and see if a short-term project could work. According to Times Jobs, more Indians are now seeking temporary employment opportunities overseas (55 per cent) rather than permanent, long-term opportunities (45 per cent) as before. Outside of the nationalism debate: 'It could be that the world is becoming less mobile. Or it could be that work itself is becoming more global, making it unnecessary for people to uproot their lives to find satisfying, well-paying jobs,' as BCG puts it. Among the latter is China, which has seen a significant dip in the willingness to go abroad, along with many central and eastern European countries, such as Poland, Croatia, Slovenia and Romania. This phenomenon is best explained by Michael Clemens of the Centre of Global Development. 'Over the course of a mobility transition,' he says, 'emigration generally rises with economic development until countries reach upper-middle income, and only thereafter falls.'

Are There New Destinations Now?

Immigration and global supply chains are inversely correlated to each other. America has benefited from low-price products from China but has also given up manufacturing roles to them. So, politicians in every country have tightened immigration policies and have put restrictions on the type and quantum of talent that a company can bring in.

This has dampened enthusiasm to work abroad.

The Indeed survey shows a 38 per cent decrease in Indians looking to move to the US and a 42 per cent decrease in those looking to work in the UK. In the US, the difficulty of obtaining green cards is pushing people to seek opportunities in Canada; Indians getting permanent residence in the latter has more than doubled since 2016. Moreover, the sore point with the US has been H-1B visas. They have consistently declined more visas to employees of Indian software exporters; in fact, companies have seen rejection rates jump from 6 per cent in 2015 to 24 per cent in 2019. US is also said to be reviewing H-4 visas that allow spouses of H-1B visa holders to work. As a fallout, many US and Indian technology companies have opened affiliate offices in Canada. The rethink on rules that allow STEM graduates to work for an additional twenty-four months following the first year after graduation in the US is swaying students to consider Canada too. The number of Indian international students studying at Canadian universities rose 127 per cent between 2016 and 2018, according to the Canadian Bureau for International Education.

Concerns and uncertainties over Brexit have impacted the UK as a potential destination. Immigration from India to the UK increased until 2012 but has since declined dramatically. Between 2012 and 2015, the number of Indians emigrating to the UK decreased from 15,00,000 to 3,25,000—an average decline of 39.9 per cent per year. It is rising again and 'experts reckon that Indians will soon become Britain's most populous migrant group once again, as the pendulum swings back to non-EU migration', says *The Economist*.

Migration for work to the Gulf has dropped by 62 per cent in the last five years. Emigration clearances granted to Indians headed to the Gulf for employment had dropped by 21 per cent to 2.95 lakh by November 2018 as compared to the same period in 2017. The economic slowdown in GCC, higher priority for nationals in both public and private sectors, and improved job prospects in India are squarely responsible.

Amidst these drops, the beneficiaries—as migration for India for employment purposes has continued to rise— are not restricted to Canada alone. India topped the list of skilled immigrants in Australia. Countries such as Germany and Ireland have seen an increase in Indians actively looking for jobs. Germany has seen a 10 per cent increase in Indians looking for jobs while Ireland has seen a 20 per cent rise. The Netherlands, Norway and Sweden, the Indeed survey says, have seen their Indian population grow by 66, 56 and 42 per cent, respectively, over seven years, till 2017.

Countries Promising Great Work–Life Balance

One of the reasons Nordic countries rank high on happiness is work-life balance. A full-time work week in Denmark is typically thirty-seven hours spread over the course of five days. On the other hand, the average American works forty-four hours per week, or 8.8 hours per day, according to the Bureau of Labor Statistics. In India, this can stretch even further. In the Netherlands, a minuscule 0.4 per cent of employees work very long hours, the lowest rate in the OECD, where the average is 11 per cent. Besides flexible work arrangements and vacation time, there's also greater focus on the wellness quotient. This, of course, fits in with the mindset of the younger employees who are keen to travel as well.

The MNC Bias

R.R. Nair says that MNCs are preferred by managers who want to work abroad because:

> There are 3–4 characteristics associated with multinationals. One is the emphasis that is given to meritocracy. Secondly, you have global systems and processes for human resource practices. Third is, people develop not only local but also global skills. Fourth is their capacity to bring in state-of-the-art technology and also basic leadership and functional competencies on a trans-national basis. It is much higher than probably [what] a local company [can do].

While offering transnational opportunities, MNCs do bring with them the dilemma of choosing between a local job and a regional or head office role. But as Nair says, in this day and age, it's important to have global experience.

> Increasingly, it is very important to have these types of exposures. Today, for example, many nationalities want to come and work in India, or even in China. Because having worked in India or China is an important requirement for them to succeed in the global marketplace.

That's no exaggeration. As McKinsey says, Asia's future is now. 'Asia is on track to top 50 per cent of global GDP by 2040 and drive 40 per cent of the world's consumption, representing a real shift in the world's centre of gravity.' Of course, China and India will have a leading role to play.

When I was in Nokia, we had so many expats coming and working in India because they felt that a stint in India or China was good on their CV. We had employees from New Zealand, Singapore, Finland and Australia working in Nokia India. The same did not happen in PepsiCo.

Anusha Shetty, chairperson and group CEO, Grey Group, India

Anusha Shetty has over twenty years of marketing and advertising experience. She has worked across India and the Silicon Valley, with agencies such as Lintas and Euro RSCG, on multiple brands, including Intel, Titan and Honeywell, among others. She co-founded Autumn Worldwide, a digital marketing firm, in 2005, which was later acquired by the Grey Group. She is now chairman and CEO, Grey Group India.

How different is it working abroad, compared to India?

From a logic and strategy perspective, there is no difference. My biggest learning was that marketing is marketing, anywhere in the world. I used to believe that the way they function would be very advanced and vastly different, but that wasn't the case. Working in the US felt like a natural transition.

From an operations perspective, it was very different. India is all about relationships and people. Work here gets done better and faster with good relationships—be it with a vendor, partner, agency, or client. On the other hand, in the US, systems and processes rule. I would upload an artwork file to a printer in another part of America, and with no follow-ups, this print consignment would reach me as per schedule. I remember another instance where we had some urgent campaign planning to complete over a weekend, and this request was made to the agency who worked with us. I directly received an invoice for the weekend work. This was the protocol followed. But coming back to India and our foundation of relationships, we always stretch an extra mile.

What made you come back to India?

Living in the US was no longer my dream. I was grateful for the exposure I had and wanted to come back to India to start a company. However, it wasn't an easy decision. I did take up a job initially until the calling became strong, and that's when I finally quit to start my own company.

You have worked with both Indian companies and MNCs. What are the advantages of working with both?

The young and new-age Indian companies are quick, agile and ready to explore. On the other hand, the older Indian companies come with a legacy and lots of love from Indians—to work with them and dream the next part of the journey is an honour.

Now with MNCs, they have the budgets. So, if we have a good idea and the patience to go through the right processes and get all the relevant approvals, everything falls into place seamlessly. Additionally, the participation of stakeholders from different countries helps expand the thinking for teams on both sides.

(Late) Chandramouli Venkatesan, former CEO (special projects), Pidilite Industries

What are the essential differences between the way Indian and multinational companies operate?

I think there is an over emphasis on ownership. But I am not sure that that is the important thing. I think there are some biases in this process. The moment we say Indian, we assume it is a family-run, promoter-led organization which is non-professional. The moment we say MNC, we automatically assume that it is a professionally run organization. These biases are not necessarily true. We could have a foreign organization that is family-run. We could have an Indian organization that is professionally run. So, in my experience what is a lot more important is the leadership of the company. It doesn't matter if the leader happens to be the owner of the company. It could be a family leader, but if the leader is a visionary and professional, it works beautifully. Sometimes you have an opposite example, where a professional leader is narrow-minded and non-progressive.

So, what is a lot more important is the quality of leadership. And what is a lot less important is whether a company is Indian or foreign. At both ends, you will find that there are great companies, average companies and poor companies. I would urge people who think about careers to ask certain questions—Is the leader progressive? Is the leadership visionary? Is it focused on the right thing? One should not have biases if the leader is the owner of the company and a permanent shareholder.

But would you say there are any significant cultural idiosyncrasies that are peculiar to MNCs and Indian companies, which govern how they operate differently from one another?

There are a lot of cultural differences. But I don't think these should be looked at from the Indian vs MNC perspective. In my opinion, even in an Indian company, there is a huge cultural difference between a company headquartered in Chennai and one headquartered in Delhi. An Infosys will not have the same culture as any other Indian corporation. So, a lot of it is company-specific factors and leadership. I mean, if you are working for Infosys, would you describe the culture as Indian or foreign? If you are working in a foreign MNC in India which has been around for a hundred years—such as Bata—would you describe that as MNC culture or Indian culture?

I find that these are convenient labels that we give. But when you dig deep, you find that not all Indian companies have the same culture, and neither do all foreign companies. There are some differences, though. The important thing when you are working in an MNC is that there is a heterogeneity of culture that you have to deal with. When you are working in an MNC and in a job which has a global interface, you do end up in a situation where, sometimes, you are working with somebody from Europe or the US. So, you can't be unidimensional in your approach. But I think this also applies to an extent in an Indian set-up. If you are a sales leader in a corporation in India, the way you motivate a salesperson in Punjab is very different from the way you do it in Kerala. If you are trying to do the same thing in both cases, it is not going to work. So, heterogeneity of culture is present in MNCs. But it is present in different ways in Indian companies as well.

At a personal level, what appealed to you more and why? What were the positives and downsides of working both for an MNC and an Indian set-up?

I didn't choose to join a company because it was Indian or because it was an MNC. It was governed by what role I was going to do, how well the company was doing, how the leaders I was engaging with were. Those were more important factors for me. I wanted to work in a good company that was progressive, had good people, people with vision and knowledge. So that is how I made my choices. I think you get tremendous learning in both. Every situation is a unique situation. In those situations, you have to adapt, irrespective of what company it is.

What do you think Indian managers are better suited for—Indian firms or MNCs, or is that very individual-dependent?

Naturally, if you are an American citizen, a born American, and you live there, you are more suited for an American company than an Indian company, and vice versa. But the issue is not what you are suitable for; what's more important is what you can adapt to. If you can't adapt, then you are going to struggle. That is true whether you are an Indian or an American or a Frenchman.

Personally, how difficult was it for you to move from an Indian company to an MNC and back again to an Indian company? Did you have to adapt to make changes according to the culture?

With every change, you have to adapt. This happens not only when you move from an Indian company to an MNC but also from MNC to MNC, or one Indian company to another. Because no two companies are the same. I think this is just convenient slotting. Every time you move, you have to adapt. I don't think it increases or decreases based on whether the shareholders are Indian or foreigners.

Vani Dandia, founder,
Cherry Peach Plum consultancy

Vani Gupta Dandia started her career with Leo Burnett, before taking a plunge into the world of brand marketing. An MBA graduate from MDI, she worked with Henkel, RB and Unilever as regional marketing manager, Hair, South Asia. Post-Unilever, she joined PepsiCo as category director, Indian Snacks and Foods, and was instrumental in the success of Kurkure. After moving on from Benddit, her previous venture, Vani launched Cherry Peach Plum, a marketing-driven management consultancy.

You moved from a national role to a regional role in Unilever when you went to work in Thailand. How difficult was the transition?

I championed the national launch of Veet for Reckitt Benckiser from 2003 to 2005. And then I moved to Unilever on a regional innovations role—the region being defined as South-East Asia plus South Asia. While my team and my boss were based in Bangkok, I was in Mumbai and travelled to Bangkok on work.

But travel aside, what was intimidating was the sheer volume of work that Unilever generated. In Unilever, at any point, there were at least twenty different live innovation projects in the pipeline. Mine, however, was called out as a high-priority project, leading the global equity transformation for Sunsilk. I was tasked to deliver the full launch mix, which included product development, packaging, pricing, portfolio and SKU strategy, consumer-validated proposition, merchandising and shelf visibility strategy, long-term pipeline, in-store promotions, and developing the full communication package. My role required me to develop this launch package and 'sell' it to the country heads of the ten different countries, convince them to launch this range in their countries, with ring-fenced investments. It was a very complex project, as I had to minimize customization for different countries, yet I had to do over thirty different artworks across a range of twelve SKUs, and I had six different languages on the back of a pack.

This was still the easy part. The difficult part was winning trust and commitment from my team. I was the only Indian, young and ambitious, very eager to make a mark at Unilever with this project, living out of a suitcase, leading the project. My team had people from Indonesia, Malaysia, Thailand, Vietnam, and a couple of Europeans/ Singaporeans who also had responsibility for some other projects. Many of my team members were much older than me. Initially, I tried doing most work over the phone from Bombay. But a month later, after four weekly project updates on the phone, I realized that something was terribly wrong. I found I was the only one talking and there was very little contribution from a team of a dozen-odd on the other end of the line. I realized that despite all my spirited talking,

I hadn't been able to 'win' the team as a project leader. I needed to spend face-to-face time with them, one on one, to really understand what was going on.

So, what was initially 'travel as needed' soon became 'a weekly red-eye flight' to Bangkok for more than three years. I started eating with my team, which meant I had to get used to the taste and smell of fish oil! As the cohesion in the team improved and we were able to understand each other better, I started to feel better about work. It was the first time that I saw the power and magic of a committed team. But it came with a lot of self-reflection, and anxiety. Competitive aggression, something we Indians are used to, is not appreciated in that part of the world. I learnt the joy of genuine collaboration and of leading by taking the back seat.

Culturally, what aspects should one keep in mind when doing a line job, compared to a staff job?

Whether it's a line or a staff job, eventually everything that any employee does must tie in with the overall goals of the organization. I didn't see myself doing a staff role in any stint—not even while I was at Unilever, when I championed the development of the innovation mix for all South-East Asia and South Asia. The challenge that big organizations face is that they are unable to bring cohesion in the way individual objectives are crafted. Some may get away with easy targets as they enjoy the patronization of some big bosses at the top and some may be too insecure to allow target-setting to be a team exercise, such that everyone is pulling together in one direction.

Looking back, would you still do the regional role or would you have stayed in the country role?

I am glad to have had the opportunity to do what I did with Unilever. It was an unparalleled experience that gave me exposure to the wider world of possibilities in so many different markets. I had to learn how to win the country teams on my side and have them believe they were co-creating the mix with me, rather than having had a launch thrust upon them. I had access to the best talent and resources in the agencies and suppliers we worked with—we used high-end technologies and printing materials that were rare in India. This role also allowed me to be at the forefront of shaping the innovation agenda for Hair with the global teams—I learnt the rationale behind prioritizing some projects over others, how to take others along, and the rigorous planning and pre-alignment needed.

I would recommend one always seek out different kinds of roles and responsibilities—the more diverse, the better. Most organizations shy away from giving critical roles to someone who doesn't have a proven track record in the same field. Still, always ask for different roles. And if you were to land something very different from what you've done before, take it up as a challenge, with the determination to excel at it!

Kirthiga Reddy, partner, SoftBank Investment Advisers, and former managing director, Facebook India and South Asia

You came to work in India and then went back to the USA. What made you decide to come back to India? What factors contributed to both decisions, moving to India and moving back to the US?

After Good Technology's acquisition by Motorola in 2007, I used to visit India often to work with the Good India division. I would see how much the country was changing—infrastructure investments, new airports, growing tech ecosystem. When an opportunity came up to lead the Good India division, I applied and was thrilled to be selected. It was a company and product I loved, working with talented people I knew well—I couldn't ask for more!

Dev and I thought we'd move back to India for a year and half and take it from there. I moved first with my two girls, Ashna and Ariya, then five and three years old. Dev got a six-month relocation approved and joined me six months later. At the end of the first year, we knew we wanted to stay longer. I joined a turnaround company, Phoenix Technology. Just as the sale of the divisions I was part of was completing, Facebook announced its intention to open an office in India.

When my girls were to start high school (ninth grade) and middle school (sixth grade), we felt that if we ever wanted to move back, that was the right window. It was a well-planned, year-long transition.

Debjani Ghosh, president, NASSCOM

You have worked outside India and then came back to India. What factors did you consider while moving out of India and then also coming back to India?

The only factor that mattered was what the role offered. Was it challenging enough to offer me the opportunity to learn, grow and increase my contribution to the company? Was it aligned to my dream of heading the India business? And would it accelerate the journey to my goal? If yes, I took the plunge.

Piyush Pandey, chief creative officer, worldwide, and executive chairman, India, O&M

You have done India roles and now you do a global role based out of India. How difficult is it for Indians to do regional or global roles, and what new capabilities do they have to adjust to?

There are so many people at Unilever, who have gone from India and have played global roles and have done a very good job of it. My thing was that I never wanted to settle outside the country. So, I was not chasing any global role. The global role came to me. I was told that I would be based out of India, so I had a very good reason to say yes. Global roles are not really difficult roles if you don't take yourself too seriously. It is impossible for any human being to know the globe the way they know their country. But it is possible to appreciate people who know their country.

So, you have to bring the team together, you have to trust them, you need to have a common goal, and, thereafter, there is no reason why you should go and tell them what to do. Get the right people and give them the empowerment they need, allowing them to set goals, and move on.

Are there any cultural challenges one faces when they go outside or handle people outside their country?

You have to respect everyone's culture. Find the people who are very proud of their culture and let them be. It is impossible to know the nuances of even Indian culture, with its diversity. When we work out of Mumbai, we find that people in Calcutta have a very different culture. So, the entire idea is to never take yourself too seriously. You must know what kind of people you respect, what kind of people you need as partners, and then move on. It is not that Virat Kohli can bowl—even he would need somebody who can bowl.

You have handled both MNC and Indian clients. How, in your opinion, are the two groups different and similar?

I think it changes from individual to individual. But earlier, with MNC clients, there used to be a format for everything, which had to be followed. But over the years, I have seen that they have also realized that they have to let go. In the '80s and '90s, MNCs were not doing great work because they were doing formats, and then they realized that your projects go with culture. So, now MNCs are doing some very good work. Look at Unilever. It is doing wonderful work from time to time. Also P&G and many others.

When it comes to locals, it is not that every local does great work. Some locals have aped the good old MNCs. And there are some very evolved people, such as Pidilite or Asian Paints, who have done great work from the early '90s on and continue to do well.

Five Things to Remember about This Dilemma

1. Going abroad was a no-brainer twenty years ago. Today, India has the size, scale and opportunity to offer talented people good roles with remunerative compensation. If you still want to go abroad, you must have a clear

reason to do so. In the past, going abroad helped you hone your skills and come back with leading-edge skills in new concept areas. That is not true anymore. The level of new knowledge and concepts is India is pretty good now.

2. India is the talent bank of the world and will be so for at least another twenty years. Talented Indians will get good roles globally, should they want it. Policies in every large, important economy are tightening to stop the flow of talented people taking away local jobs.

3. The countries of choice in the past were the US and the UK. Now, especially with millennials, quality of life and work-life balance are important factors, and we see the rise of Canada, Australia, New Zealand and the Nordic countries as destinations for work.

4. India is a top-ten market for most good MNCs. Going abroad with an MNC, either to a regional role or a head-office role, only makes sense if it is part of a larger career picture. So, do think that through. The worst thing to do is to go and do a desk job which no one will value here in India when you get back. Do not forget to keep in touch with headhunters and senior managers in India when you are away. That's your return visa in most cases.

5. You have to be clear whether you are going to uproot your family, if you have a one-way ticket to work abroad. It is a lot to ask from the family if you are unsure about what the next steps are. Be clear even

if you are going to the subsidiary of a multinational. There are many things that are different about different subsidiaries, and you should not regret that you didn't do your homework.

Dilemma 8

Should I Turn Entrepreneur?

Every executive is bitten by this bug of wanting to go solo. The bug comes from many different directions, but maybe the most important is not being driven by the vision of the company where they work. When that spark is not there, then executives want to start out on their own.

A good many executives drop out of the corporate rat race by the time they are in their early forties. They recognize that it is a hard grind and they are better off on their own. The most common thing to do is to start a consultancy. Whether you should take the plunge or not—that is the dilemma.

How does one think about this dilemma?

The Big Picture

There are twenty-four unicorns in India, according to NASSCOM. Some galloped their way into the club over the last decade, seven of them in 2019 alone. The numbers—propelled by Internet businesses as they took root—also fuelled the growing entrepreneurial ambitions in India. In 2018, about 63.7 per cent of Indians considered entrepreneurship to be a desirable career choice, higher than the global average of 62.4 per cent, as per the Global Entrepreneurship Monitor. Borrowing the industry body's words, both had approached 'escape velocity'. Technology and the Internet are the enablers—with these you don't need a visiting card, nor an office; all you need is a website and a cellphone, and you are good to go.

IT firms and multinationals were the places to work at for the ambitious. Entrepreneurship was by and large unappealing, the prerogative of communities with established ecosystems or large business families. The early start-ups sprouted and spread in e-commerce, food delivery, ride hailing, digital payments, and more. Entrepreneurship also brought about societal change. The frenzy was evident in the media, with talks revolving around valuations, funding, global investors and M&A deals. The intent gained momentum as many were willing to venture out of their stable jobs, sometimes straight out of college and even leadership positions, to try out their business ideas.

I remember every time I spoke at an Indian business school in the 2000–15 era, students would come up and ask me which companies and sectors they should join on the basis of their interest. Whenever I spoke at US business schools—Harvard, Kellogg and suchlike—students would go one step further to ask me, 'Shiv, I have this idea for a product or service, what do you think about it?' However, I do see that there are many more students on campus who want to try their hand at entrepreneurship now.

Walmart paying $16 billion to acquire a 77 per cent share of Flipkart has been a game changer. The euphoria is now fading somewhat because of governance issues plus the progress made. Indian entrepreneurs tend to put monies behind advertising and do a lot of public relations. This creates a larger-than-life company and opportunity. Many are falling by the wayside.

The normal and proper filter of questions is along the lines of—What's the strategy? What consumer or customer problem are we trying to solve? Do we have the right capital, the right talent and the right business model to succeed? These are not looked into diligently, which is why woolly concepts and woolly-headed thinking fails every day.

Stung by failures and uncertainty, many are returning to the fold of stable jobs and assignments. Questions are being asked on business feasibility. The strategy of 'discounts and promotions' is being called out. *What if this private capital were to run dry?*—this is an echo from several quarters. The valuations are correcting, there is focus on downsizing and on the way to go public. All of this has compounded the dilemma: Is it a good idea to become an entrepreneur?

Evolution

Looking back, it was the IT companies that changed the rules. There are stories of how Infosys was bootstrapped after its founders broke away from Patni Systems. Others followed in a similar fashion, making IT an enabler, a nurturing ground for entrepreneurs in the '80s. In today's context, the quintessential example is of the Bansals, former Amazon employees, who founded Flipkart. Three employees of Flipkart, in turn, have set up the B2B trading platform named Udaan. Stories abound of these entrepreneurial journeys; each instance, each iteration shows how the start-up universe has expanded, closely in sync with digital growth in India.

The country has evolved from being the IT, services and outsourcing hub into a significant R&D centre. The increase in expendable income has amplified its potential, bringing in international investment and focus, aiding the entrepreneurial journeys. India now has 80,000 start-ups, according to Bain & Company. They raised $10 billion in 2019, up from $3.1 billion in 2012. 'That puts India's venture capital activity behind America ($114 billion) and China ($34 billion) but ahead of larger economies such as Germany or France,' says *The Economist*. Many of these are advanced technology start-ups, working with data analytics, artificial intelligence, and the Internet of Things. From hyperlocal deliveries to e-commerce, the focus has shifted to B2B models and deep-tech, IP-driven innovation. Start-up hubs are developing in tier-I and tier-II cities, but the focus is no longer just local.

Contrary to perception, the founders aren't 'young, fresh college graduates' either. Studies show the median age is closer to late twenties and thirties. Armed with multiple degrees and experiences under their belt, their ambitions are far away from tethering a job.

'Despite the stability in jobs and the benefits of high salaries and other perks, they (founders) perceived jobs as constraining their creativity,' says an Observer Research Foundation (ORF) study. 'A lack of identification with corporate culture often leads them to create something on their own, which enables them to define their own values and control their own direction.' This yearning to build is what many founders describe as the reason for their plunge.

The path to entrepreneurship, though, is harsh. Trying to establish a brand, battling bigger competitors and keeping business profitable is difficult, no matter how many years you've worked. This lack of experience can be one's undoing, says Balaraman V., founder of Boardroom Advantage.

> If it is someone who is totally raw, becoming an entrepreneur would be an uphill task. I think one needs to be rough and tough by working for other companies. One has to be mature and know people. If you do not know people, you can never be a businessman. You have to know people, know how to understand people, how to work with them, how to work for them, how to work below them, how to work along with them. That requires a little bit of exposure. It requires an experience of the world, so work in a few companies before starting out to get some maturity.

Challenges

IBM's 2016 report says that 90 per cent of Indian start-ups fail within the first five years, citing lack of innovation as the main reason for shutting shop. While this is true, start-ups are evolving from simply emulating Western concepts in India to building unique products, going beyond consumer to B2B marketplaces, health-tech, enterprise-tech, robotics, fin-tech and more. The struggle, even today, is more about funding, which inadvertently means overlooking customer performance metrics, sales and profitability.

The ORF study shows that, while raising funds has become easier, the majority of start-ups are 'bootstrapped and not self-sufficient, but struggle to obtain funds, although they can show a proof of concept and some market validation'. Getting early-stage funding is critical for start-ups to build a prototype, run tests, get key employees on board and acquire their initial set of customers. In 2018, ORF says, the seed stage funding dropped by 40 per cent compared to a year earlier.

Reasons for Startup Failure According to Venture Capitalists

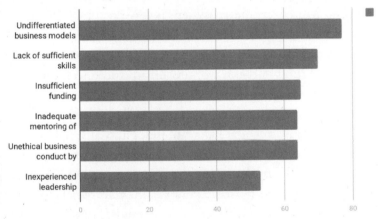

Between 2011 and 2015, multiple venture capitalists (VCs) entered India, attracted to the rapid activity taking place. The blind bullishness meant many 'burnt money'. The course correction that followed saw VCs fund more mature start-ups, which already have an MVP (minimum viable product) and some proven market traction. Also, money came on a trust basis, which meant that funds were disbursed among known circles and based on familiarity and similarity, not diversity. Getting Series A and B funding is still hard for companies, barring the larger names.

Over the past two years, however, the VC industry in India has been in a renewed growth phase. 'Currently, of the almost 80,000 start-ups in India, only about 8 per cent are funded, indicating room for investments,' says Bain. Barely a few start-ups have paying customers to be sustainable and grow organically. With the ongoing price wars for the discount-happy Indian consumer and competition at the heels, many businesses are volume-driven, with negative returns. Moreover, the ecosystem is less favourable to start-ups that develop hardware or other physical products. It's the tech basket that has most of the eggs. 'Many investors chase trends and fund start-ups working on advanced technologies, which, despite a few interesting use cases, have low relevance to solving more urgent Indian problems,' says ORF.

It's not just a capital hang-up, though, that's making the lives of entrepreneurs difficult. It is important as a founder to engage with investors who bring value beyond funding. Can these investors facilitate your vision? Can they help with customer acquisition or open up new market opportunities? These are questions that founders need to figure out. Investors predominantly fund start-ups, looking to exit within a few years with multiple times the initial amount invested. Few have a more long-term orientation and are willing to invest in R&D-intense start-ups. The exit strategy can dilute the influence of founders; some may even find themselves out of a job. 'Between 20 and 40 per cent of founders do not remain in their original role, typically replaced by a more-seasoned executive who might seem better positioned to scale the company and prepare it for the acquisition or IPO market,' says *Harvard Business Review*. Scaling up is a challenge of mammoth proportions, where each step needs to be measured. Entrepreneurs often lament the absence of a support system, a sounding board to troubleshoot problems.

Navigating the Maze Is a Challenge

For new founders, coming from professional backgrounds, accelerators, incubators and mentorship programmes can mean the difference between success and failure. India today has over 300 incubators and accelerators. They offer everything—mentorship, office space, networks for elite talent and investors, exposure trips, and more. Microsoft, Walmart Labs, Qualcomm Technologies, SAP, Shell and others run accelerator programmes. There are a slew of new ones, such as YC, Techstars, Entrepreneur First and Sequoia, betting on India. Indian firms—from Yes Bank to Reliance Jio and Airtel—are joining the wave, as are the central and state governments. The latter, start-ups say, can do much more to aid their journey. States such as Kerala and Telangana have better programmes to grow entrepreneurs led by smart ministers and bureaucrats.

The bureaucratic process is still a challenge. The continuous changes in regulation can mean pivoting business models, or at the very least, finding workarounds to the problem at hand. In a survey of 33,000 start-ups, over 80 per cent say they have received no benefit from Startup India, and over 50 per cent say that the single biggest challenge to business remains governance and bureaucratic inefficiency.

There are plenty of inefficiencies in-house, too. In spite of funding rounds and big hires, unicorns have struggled to keep their costs under check, forcing them to lay off employees across teams. This has worsened during the pandemic. Others are no better. Their reasons range from restructuring of operations, to reducing costs and fund crunch. Around 3200 employees were laid off from their roles across six different unicorns in 2019, according to *Mint*. This has diminished the lure of start-ups. Randstad's 2019 survey shows 55 per cent of Indians prefer to work for multinationals, while just 9 per cent prefer start-ups. Besides, start-ups can rarely compete with the compensation structures that large companies offer.

In between finding the right talent and reducing costs and fund crunch, the HR tussles are many. Gender bias is one. A report by Bain and Google shows the potential loss at hand. 'There are an estimated 16 million women-owned and controlled enterprises, representing approximately 20 per cent of all enterprises today that are creating direct employment for about 27 million people in India.' They can generate 150-170 million jobs by 2030, which is more than 25 per cent of the new jobs required for the entire working-age population. That's something to address but the biggest question being raised is profitability, or the lack of it, of Indian start-ups. Investors see only secondary exits in the near term in India. Valuations are 'marked to myth', which makes public listings or private sales rare, says *The Economist*. It's not alone. Many are flagging the chinks in the booming start-up scene—one where, NASSCOM says, there are fifty-two more unicorns in the works.

I would like you to take a shot at this dilemma in a structured manner:

1. Do I have a good business idea that solves a genuine need in society, or do I have a copycat idea which is late to the market? Copycat ideas have no choice of success. The biggest copycat ideas I see are in management consulting, marketing consulting, digital marketing agencies and the next 'different' advertising agency. I have seen so many friends go down this route with little success.

2. There is a tendency for a few friends to sit together over a drink and cobble up a company. Avoid this tendency of thinking that good friends make good partners at work. Disagreements with founding partners is among the top three reasons for failure of start-ups. So, friends should maybe stay friends, and not become partners. Friends turning foes is an instant two-minute recipe for disaster.

3. Start-ups work best in an ecosystem where they work with large companies in the industry. The German and US ecosystems are good examples. India is still some distance away from that situation. So, try and find a large company to work with.

4. Don't run the start-up with the only strategy being that a large company will acquire you. I know of two beverage companies that have been in this mode for a few years now, and nothing has come out of it. COVID-19 has taken the wind out of the sails of these two companies.

5. Gujarat has been a hot bed of entrepreneurship. Gujarati entrepreneurs have given MNCs a run for their money in categories such as tea, ice cream, deodorants. Having travelled and worked the Gujarat market many times and interacted with consumers, I can say that Gujarati entrepreneurs and consumers have a nose for high-quality products at the right value point. Wagh Bakri, Havmor, Avva, Fogg and Nirma are good examples.

6. Get a good sounding board if you are starting on your own. You must pick someone who is willing to challenge you and tell you the truth.

7. India is not at the stage when failed entrepreneurs are welcomed back to the mainstream job market. This is an important change we need as a society. Till we embrace failure as a learning experience, we will not really give entrepreneurs the confidence of a safety net.

Anusha Shetty, chairperson and group CEO, Grey Group, India

How difficult is it to be an entrepreneur?

The word 'difficult' never occurred to me. I just knew I wanted to do it. Hard work becomes much easier when the dream is real. Did I have bad days? Yes, I definitely did. I would always choose to sleep on it and allow myself the chance to wake up to a bright new day.

What were the highs and lows of your journey?

The biggest high in this journey is the work and doing what I love. Seeing your work come to life, clients winning, being acknowledged for great work and colleagues bursting with pride—there is no bigger high than this. Growth and money followed good work, and that was the icing on the cake.

The initial few years were easy. There was no benchmark and everything was good. Then you reach a phase when you are not small, yet not big enough to have everything work in your favour. You don't have the funds to hire senior talent, you don't have the funds for marketing, your network is limited and suddenly, you feel stuck. Not being able to grow when you have the right intentions and commitment can be extremely daunting. I faced it, but then one day, it just pops and everything is different, it's better. The only takeaway is to never give up and always do your best because results do follow.

Do you need mentors on the journey? Who were your mentors and what help did they give you?

Yes, mentors are a must. Being a founder and leader, teams expect you to solve all their problems. But then you are human too and, sometimes, you need a shoulder to lean on.

There is no better partner than a mentor. I have been blessed in this area. Mr Balaraman (ex-CEO, Pond's Unilever) was my early mentor. From branding or strength from the power of the world—we could discuss everything. I walked away always feeling stronger. Then I met Mr Ravishankar, who stood by me through the last ten years, teaching me to read a balance sheet, manage my cash, hold ethical grounds on finance, and so much more. Under his guidance, I grew Autumn Worldwide until it was acquired by Grey, a WPP company. I still call him for advice. I would not be who I am, without my mentors.

How did you collect your senior management team?

Sixty per cent of my senior management team grew with me. They were young and fresh at Autumn, and we grew together. Now they hold senior management roles in the company. The rest of the senior management joined me much later. I still remember one of them inviting himself to an interview. He had done his homework on Autumn and was there to tell me why I should hire him. I went silent on him later as I had to think about investments on talent, but he wouldn't give up. He asked to see me again and I loved that perseverance and commitment. I also loved his POV on digital, and sure enough, he was on board. I have been extremely fortunate to have many of the teams that grew with Autumn stay on for many years to continue supporting the dream as seniors. Many people even moved on from the organization, only to come back to Autumn with more experience, perspectives and a renewed determination.

You decided to sell your firm to Grey, part of WPP. How difficult was that decision?

It wasn't difficult to let go. I was clear that we would scale greater heights with this acquisition. I also knew my teams needed larger wings to fly far and high. What was difficult was choosing the right partner. It's like an arranged marriage where the obvious reasons are out and open, but you know that real marriage comes with real connections and lies in the nuances. This was a perfect choice with Grey WPP.

Harish Devarajan, leadership coach

What made you turn entrepreneur when many companies would have snapped you up as an HR head?

I had the option to go back to Unilever UK to head either the European business as an HR head or take on one of the corporate roles in HR. I turned down the option and decided to get started on my own. I don't know whether I can call myself an entrepreneur; I call myself one of the early gig professionals in India. I got into the economy pretty early. I was forty-six. A lot of colleagues and friends asked me why I was ending my career. It was on a couple of counts.

One, I felt that I did not have enough balance in life. I was one-dimensional. I was focused on my corporate career, which is what most of my colleagues across companies spent a lot of time doing. As an HR person, I had seen that we would go out and recruit people who were all-rounders. Every single person that I recruited at Hindustan Lever had multiple talents. We made them unidimensional robots. We hardly gave them any time to develop and pursue other talents. And at sixty, when they were superannuated, they came back and asked if they could still continue to consult for the company. I didn't want to get stuck in that. I was very clear that the moment I felt I was secure from a financial perspective, I would allocate my time to other things.

The decision created a balance. Family, which had taken a backseat, started becoming important. I say this to a lot of people today. I read a quote a couple years before I actually took this call, I don't know whose quote this is, but it said: 'You've missed the growth of your children whilst you were busy focusing on the growth in your profession.' It had a big impact on my belief system.

Second, I decided I would pursue an aspect of my profession that I enjoy the most. So, I took on coaching, working with those who were interested in improving themselves. I also decided that it would take up only a third of my time and that I was not going to work twenty-two days a month as I had for the last twenty-five years. I decided to spend time with organizations which needed help but could not afford it, such as NGOs, pro bono. I also work with organizations trying to transform themselves, which is where I spent another third of my time. So, coaching and consulting is what I do for money. But I spend a significant amount of my time with the NGO and social sector. And I spend a lot of time with my family. I travel and follow my passions, including networking, theatre, dance, reading, writing, etc. I'm on my second book now. These things have now become a reality after becoming an entrepreneur.

Becoming an entrepreneur has its insecurities. You have to rely on friends or networks to initially get a kick-start. How difficult is it to ask for business from people who have been your friends?

I am not great at marketing by myself. I never went to my friends to say 'give me some work'. What I did is I shared what I wanted to do with my network, both friends and associates. Quite a few people did reach out in the initial days, offering me jobs. A lot of people—friends and CEOs of companies—offered me jobs and asked me to join their company as an HR head. The papers also spread news of me joining Infosys or the Tata group as HR head. They reached out but I was very clear about what I wanted. Many of them realized what I was keen on doing and ended up offering me engagements, and that kept flowing in. When you do one job in the space of coaching, the network reaches out to you because they have seen something positive. So, in an indirect way, friends and networks give you early opportunities that get you started.

How big should entrepreneurs dream?

There are two sides to this. One, as an entrepreneur you have to dream of the impossible. This is when you become relevant. If you want to do what is already done, your relevance is very limited. You have got to be offering something which people aspire for and do not have experience of. From that point of view, an entrepreneur must dream of the impossible.

Having said that, you no longer have the comfort of resources you are used to when you work in large organizations. Suddenly, you are the master of your time and space, and you are the resource available for making things happen. To me, I was the only resource. But even the quality of resources you will have to hire in the initial stages will be far different from what you are used to in organizations such as Unilever or Tata. Definitely, you will have to live within your constraints. It is a form of art. Dream big and be aware of your constraints; it makes you behave in a very different way. It makes you realize that you do not need to own all the resources, but you can leverage your resources through many different mechanisms. You then break out of the framework you are used to and start finding new ways for achieving your goals rather than to dictate, decide and direct. That's what entrepreneurship is all about. It is about finding the new world, the new method and a new reality.

What do you miss about the corporate world? You spoke about resources, but even at a personal level, what do you miss about your job?

First is the network. A company is not only about resources but also about the friends, companions and mentors you have. You can walk in and have a conversation anytime with anyone and then walk out, and it will give you food for thought. All entrepreneurs talk about the same thing—*it is the quality of conversations that we miss.*

Second, of course, are the resources that are available. And third is, whom do I turn to when I am stuck? The inability to get help to unlock some roadblocks is a difficulty. I always encourage people to create their own buddy group, and not necessarily inside the organization. Go outside your organization. Continue to nurture the mentor relationships you have with the people you have worked with in the past. Make a new network of friends outside the immediate organization. It is not easy, it takes time. These are amongst the many things you have to do by yourself. That's what one really needs when you move out of the corporate world and into entrepreneurship.

Meena Ganesh, serial entrepreneur & CEO, Portea Medical

Meena Ganesh is one of India's most successful entrepreneurs, with nearly three decades of experience in industries such as healthcare, consulting, technology, outsourcing, education and e-commerce. She is CEO, Portea Medical, which brings in-home care to patients—geriatric, chronic, post-operative—as well as allied healthcare services. Till February 2013, Meena was a promoter and board member of Tutor Vista, and CEO and MD, Pearson Education Services. Prior to her stint with Pearson, Meena set up the Tesco Hindustan Service Centre and was also the only Indian and among only four women in the Global Retail Council of Tesco. Meena previously also co-founded Customer Asset, a BPO company which she sold to ICICI OneSource. She has had previous stints with Microsoft India, PricewaterhouseCoopers and NIIT. Meena is a PGDM holder from IIM Calcutta and has a graduate degree in physics from Madras University.

You've been a serial entrepreneur. How and why did you decide to become one?

I founded my first start-up in 2000 when I was working with Microsoft in India and had opportunity to interact with a number of software companies. We had developed perfect technologies for their products. I felt like I ought to be an entrepreneur, but I also didn't just want to be working with start-ups in the software development or the technology field, because there were a lot of companies doing that. I didn't have a particular niche that I wanted to focus on. So, I decided to start with customer management, and that led to the founding of Customer Asset in 2000.

What was it specifically that led you down this path? You had a very successful corporate career. Was it something that was lacking in your corporate job, or was it just an inherent bug that bit you at that time?

It was a bit of both. My husband was an entrepreneur even before that—since 1990. So, I had an inside view of what the challenges of being an entrepreneur were; it was not new to me. Talking to a lot of entrepreneurs in the software phase also made me realize that I wanted to be part of that space. And in all the corporate work that I did, it was always intrapreneurial—setting up a new department or setting up a new function altogether or a new business line; that had been my journey ever since I started my job in 1985. To some degree, the whole concept of building something from nothing was already known to me and it was something I enjoyed. But till then, I had done that within the ambit of an organization. So that gave me confidence and a desire to do something on my own. Also, I had been a part of large organizations, and felt I needed to be a part of something smaller and more impactful where I could make a difference.

You've had this journey not once, but several times. What are the peculiar challenges that you have faced every time you have undertaken this entrepreneurial journey?

The whole journey of an entrepreneur is challenging. It is always evolving, as something that you think will pan out in a certain way doesn't and things unexpectedly change. This happened right from my very first start-up. In 2000, there was a meltdown, and we suddenly had to completely change what we were supposed to do. Throughout the journey there were challenges, there were pivots, there were great successes and lots of failures.

Could you elaborate a little bit on some of the most common challenges that all start-ups face?

The first challenge is to get the product right. Then somebody should want to pay for whatever you are trying to offer. Next thing is that you need to get investors around you to believe that it is something which has value in it. Then you need people who are willing to work with you in a start-up setting.

What advice would you give to first-time professional entrepreneurs? What is an absolute prerequisite for somebody entering this space?

First, you need to be very clear that it is something you want to do. You need to be passionate and really crazy about it. Irrespective of what others advise you or whatever research you do, it takes thrice the time, effort and money than what you would have thought about while starting. So, you'd better be very, very clear because you are going to be in it for the long haul. You need to make it work, make it relevant to customers and keep generating value, which is the most important thing. But it gives you great satisfaction when you look back and see that you have created a whole new category, given jobs for so many people, impacted so many people's lives. That is the positive side, but for building all of that, a lot of hard work and unexpected ups and downs are involved, which you need to be ready for.

Sujatha Duvvuri, co-founder & chief product officer, SHEMADE Gourmet Foods

Sujatha Duvvuri has had an unusual career graph. She graduated in International Economics from the University of Michigan, Ann Arbor in 2002, and chose to remain a stay-at-home mom to her kids for the next twelve years. Being fiercely particular about what they ate, she began experimenting with a host of homemade food products for her kids. In 2016, after the kids had grown up, she decided she wanted to turn entrepreneur and expand her consumer base beyond her kids and close friends. That's when she founded SHEMADE Gourmet Foods, a company that makes food that belongs to the 'free-from' category.

You finished studying at the University of Michigan, Ann Arbor and went on to become an entrepreneur. Why did you choose entrepreneurship and not a job?

I was very clear I did not want to be in a job. Right after I graduated, I had my first child. One of the things that I wanted to do was stay home and be with my child, spend time with him, watch him grow up, and control his food and nutrition. Somewhere along the journey, just as I was taking care of all of this, I thought about doing something related to food, and that's how the entrepreneur was born.

I didn't know what exactly I wanted to do. Many people in my family, including my husband, said that graduating from University of Michigan and attending campus interviews but not actually taking up a job was a very stupid decision. But I was very clear. I always wanted to do something on my own.

So, where did this entrepreneurial bug bite you?

I was just hands-on with my son first, and then with my daughter, about food and very picky about little things that would go into their meal, such as macro and micro nutrients, and so on. In spite of being an economist, I was totally drawn, in terms of my interest, towards food.

What are some of the difficulties of starting up as an entrepreneur?

When I started on this journey, I had no idea how big or small I wanted to be, or which direction I was headed in. I started baking at home first for my kids and then for my friends. It spread through word of mouth. One thing led to another and soon I was at a point where I was expected to produce so much more than I could deliver. I just didn't know how to go about it. I guess that's where the right mentor, right guidance, good wishes and a whole bunch of people helped as an entrepreneur.

How difficult was it to raise funding?

It was difficult. There were also difficulties in trying to scale the business as a first-time entrepreneur. I got my seed capital very easily. But then, the consecutive rounds were very difficult because I had to find a VC or an individual investor who totally understood food. Most VCs I would go to for funding had either funded someone in the seed round and were waiting to fund them in consecutive rounds, or they were only interested in tech start-ups because those were more mass-oriented and that's where they could see a lot of returns.

Gluten-free, given the population of India and the kind of knowledge that people had, was something that the VCs didn't see as a space that would give them returns very soon. So, there was constantly a struggle, going to a fund house for funding. I've been lucky when I've gone to individuals and really explained my proposition and the concept, and how it will catch up. But it has been a struggle.

One of the interesting aspects of doing a job is that you are constantly learning from your peers and your networks. Entrepreneurship can be a very lonely journey. So, how do you keep learning as an entrepreneur since you don't have people, especially bosses or mentors, to teach you?

I've had the right mentors from day one. I've been extremely lucky. Some mentors tell you what to do. Some teach you as you go along. They show you the way. I felt that since I started this entrepreneurship journey right after my undergrad, and I didn't go on to get a management degree from a business school, I lacked the skills that an entrepreneur needs to have to run a business. But luckily, and I keep telling Shiv this, all his YouTube videos were pretty much like an MBA degree for me. So, yes, I have learnt.

My husband has been a constant source of encouragement. In a family, if there is one entrepreneur, you are always worried about how the house is going to run, and who's going to pay the bills. But my husband has been a pillar of support on that front and a critic as well. You need certain critics as well. You don't always want someone appreciating you and saying things you like to hear. My son, of course, has been playing the perfect role of someone who gives me the right opinion on a product. There is so much that I have learnt from the feedback that I get from him. There is a lot of learning and assessment that comes from different places, and I am constantly learning from everyone, including other brands and the consumer. I am not simply giving them what I want. I am actually learning about their needs and then developing something based on that.

Do you think it's important for somebody in the family to have a steady job while one pursues entrepreneurship? Is that an important back-up?

Yes, it is. It also depends on the age of the entrepreneur. If the entrepreneur is very young, in their early twenties, obviously the person is taking a lot of risk. In my case, I did this at a much later stage in life. My husband was well established and came with a lot of experience and support.

Vani Dandia, founder,
Cherry Peach Plum consultancy

You were doing well and could have continued your corporate life; what made you turn entrepreneur?

The twenty years of corporate life were so hectic, I felt I'd packed in fifty years' worth! I've headed global and local brands, landed pure play innovation mixes, and also country functional revenue roles, worked with regional and multi-cultural teams, done advertising, marketing and GM (general manager) roles, changed seven companies and several jobs . . . so I felt I really had seen and done it all.

I always found the entrepreneurial world really alluring. I loved the bravado, the newness of the things they dabbled with, the zip-zap-zoom energy and pace of work—I was hooked! I now work with different companies as an external head of marketing, executing solutions that deliver business growth.

What variables did you consider when you decided to turn entrepreneur?

How much do I have in the bank—if I were to make nothing a couple of months, would I get by? Would I be comfortable working alone? You don't have office colleagues to hang out with, or a team that you can lean on. Would I be able to sustain the drive and ambition to succeed alone, without being a part of a large structure? Can I manage lull periods? I learnt from Sanjeev Bikhchandani that, in entrepreneurship, there is no such thing as a failure until one decides to give up. So long as one doesn't give up, one is simply 'not yet successful'. I find this premise very motivating.

Other questions were: Can I do without the comfort of a title? When one has a pretty CXO title, everyone flocks to you, sends you invites for events, is happy to sponsor expensive trips, lavish you with privileges, etc. When one turns entrepreneur, one must get used to being treated very differently.

You posted that you have given up your driver and your credit card to ensure that your costs were kept to a minimum. Is this easy to do or difficult?

As an entrepreneur, when there is no visibility to a regular stream of income, it is best to keep costs to a minimum. Ever since the idea of turning entrepreneur came to me, I knew I'd have to change my lifestyle. I had, at one time, intended to buy a house, and I saw several properties in the complex I'm currently living in. But having done the math with my financial advisors, I realized that living in a rented apartment made more financial sense. Similarly, I started monitoring my credit card bill, and cut back on a lot of discretionary spending. I haven't, however, reduced spending on all that I most love—travelling and art, for instance.

What is the joy in being an entrepreneur?

It's a sense of being completely in control, of driving one's own agenda and calendar, of working with great speed to 'deliver' rather than to 'prove I'm right', of challenging the old ways of working, of experimenting and learning. Large corporates struggle to offer you this agility, flexibility and empowerment—no matter what they say about their culture, vision or corporate practices.

Who gives you business when you start as an entrepreneur? Your old company? Your old friends? Or good Samaritans who believe in you?

It's one's network of friends and well-wishers that sets your boat afloat in the early stages. Having said that, my first few projects came as cold calls from LinkedIn—I responded to the queries I received for advice, and those converted to business. And I continue to get work from both my own network as well as from the industry.

Hari Menon, co-founder, Big Basket

Hari Menon is an accidental entrepreneur. Prior to starting Big Basket, he co-founded Fabmart, one of the pioneers in e-commerce in India. He was CEO, Indiaskills—the vocational education joint venture between Manipal Group and City & Guilds (UK), and served as country head, Planet Asia. Hari has also had a stint with Wipro as business head in the infotech business. He is an alumnus of BITS Pilani.

You started as an entrepreneur in retail very early . . .

I wasn't thinking of becoming an entrepreneur. It happened during a series of meetings that we (my colleague and I) were having with a bank while we were working with Planet Asia, bidding to build India's first payment gateway. The bank asked us —what's the point in having a gateway, we also need to have a transacting site. So, the bank decided that they'll also build a transacting site, just to enhance the concept. That was the whole idea and then, a week later, the bank was told by their headquarters that they should not enter the business of creating any transacting website. So the whole thing fell apart. But we realized that there was an opportunity. We were working with Planet Asia, which was basically an Internet services company. We thought this was probably a chance for us to do something. And that was the moment of truth. We decided to build that site and then build the payment gateway. That is how we got working on our first entrepreneurial journey, which was to build a company called Fabmart, India's first e-commerce portal.

You and your friends have stuck it out through thick and thin, when commonly we see many entrepreneurs break up. What is the secret and how do you resolve disagreements?

The single biggest thing in this is trust. I keep telling people that it is one of the key ingredients that founders must be aware of. Because you'll go through ups and downs, you'll go through tough situations when you have to manage your home, manage people externally and manage employees. It's very critical that the founders stay together, especially when they are going through tough times. The thing that really drew us all together was the fact that we just trusted each other.

   We do have professional differences all the time. We differ on many things as far as business is concerned. But at the end of the day, we just go ahead with what is right. Once we decide to go ahead, there's no 'I'm not happy with the decision, because it didn't go in my favour'. At the core of all this is the fact that there is trust. So, I am never worried about somebody else doing something behind my back.

With Big Basket, you're now into a predominantly digital venture. Can you lay out the differences in

entrepreneurship between running something in a physical world versus running a digital start-up?

There's no difference. An entrepreneur is an entrepreneur. Businesses could differ; they could be digital or physical, or a combination of both. Everyone is talking about omni-channel right now in India. So, it doesn't matter what business you are in. Entrepreneurship doesn't change too much; the basic ingredients of an entrepreneur, which is an ability to take risks, being nimble, etc., are all the same.

Any advice for young entrepreneurs?

The first important thing is to make sure that your ecosystem is ready for whichever business you are in. I'm saying that because I've got a lot of experience regarding this. When we started Fabmart, there was no ecosystem. We didn't have broadband and the Internet was slow. There weren't any payment gateways, no logistics networks. So, a lot of Internet businesses at that time were set up on hype. The ecosystem is now ready and that makes all the difference.

Second is, don't optimize too much when you begin on valuations and stake-holding. It's important to raise capital for the long term, for a minimum runway of three years. Capital is the most difficult thing. If you don't have a source of money and you are in the market, you'll never build a business. This is what people end up doing—they raise lesser capital than they need, and falter. And third is, build a good founding team based on trust.

Five Things to Remember about This Dilemma

1. Start with a good product idea or service idea that is unique and differentiated. Starting with a copycat idea and relying on hope as a strategy is not sound entrepreneurship.

2. Entrepreneurship is getting a significant boost because of the Internet and platform thinking. India has so many informal markets that can be aggregated with technology to provide transparency and better governance.

3. Entrepreneurship needs a talented team, adequate capital and a good sounding board. Friends can turn foes when you start something together. Resist that temptation till you are clear right at the outset as to how you will address disagreements between the founders.

4. Many states in India can do a lot more to help entrepreneurship. Kerala and Telangana are definitely two states that are doing some good work to encourage entrepreneurship.

5. Have an experienced sounding board to challenge you and to tell you the truth, no matter how bitter the truth is.

Dilemma 9

To Join or Not Join a Board

India has the maximum number of listed companies in the world, a little over 5000 on the BSE. Every listed company needs independent directors, many companies have advisory boards, many institutions have a board of governors/directors. Hence there is enough opportunity for a talented professional to contribute as a board member.

Arumugham Mahendran, a successful serial entrepreneur and former MD, Godrej Consumer Products, had a good quip about board directors. He said, 'Every chairman wants like-minded directors on the board, that is, directors who like his mind!'

I have been on close to a dozen boards—listed companies, advisory boards and educational institutions—and I have learnt a lot from my colleagues on the board as also the way a company or institution runs. Being on a board has developed me holistically. These are the lessons I have amassed from the experience:

1. Invitation to join a board can happen via headhunters, via the CEO, via friends. When I was being considered for the Godrej Consumer Products board, they invited me to do a two-hour session on 'innovation' to the board. Many headhunters have approached me over the years for board roles but I had to decline them as most multinational companies allow you one board position. You need to develop a network if you want to be on boards.

2. When invited to join the board of a company, do your homework well. Read up extensively about the company, the chairman of the board, other board members and the CEO. Accept the board seat only when you are sure that the company has good governance and that you will contribute and learn. One has to commit time to a board; one cannot be an absentee member or a silent member. A great board can add value to a company and contribute to its reputation. The worst thing is to be seen as a rubber stamp of the chairman.

3. The role of the lead director is pivotal; he/she leads the oversight process. Bharat Doshi of Mahindra Group was the lead director on the Godrej board, and I learnt a lot from him in the way he addressed audit issues and potential divergent points of view with the chairman. He was always respectful and honest in dealing with disagreements. He would ask the auditors one last question in every audit meeting with the independent directors: 'Is there anything that the company is asking you to do which you think the independent directors should know?'

4. When you are the chairman of the board, you have to recognize that your role is to support the CEO, not to do his/her job. Where I have been chairman, I have taken care to ensure that I am well connected with the CFO, company secretary and CEO, to ensure smooth working of the board with my colleagues. The worst thing for an operating company is to have the chairman and board members rain down on them like a ton of bricks. The chairman should play a balancing role in the disagreements.

5. A big challenge for every board member is to keep the balance between being strategic and digging into detail. I have found that the best boards are strategic, focusing on direction, people, succession and bringing in fresh thinking to the company. Boards lose their effectiveness when they become too detail-oriented and get involved in the nitty-gritty. Staying true to the board role and purpose is everyone's role. The challenge for every board member is to be constructive and not chase the leadership team into rabbit holes in search of irrelevant detail.

6. Boards can play an excellent role in M&As (mergers and acquisitions) because of the experience they bring as also their ability to look at the acquisition objectively from a distance. Many poorly thought out acquisitions have been stopped at the board's doorstep.

7. Board members can add value in the board sub-committees. New topics, such as sustainability, technology, CSR, are all good areas for contribution.

8. Confidentiality is paramount when you are a board member and I have seen many stories of other boards and

companies traded during lunch sessions. This is something one has to be careful about as a board member—you can talk about what's in the public domain but not about things that are likely to have some impact either on business or informal reputation.

9. Advisory boards do not have the legal accountability of boards but serve as a great vehicle for the leadership team to get a good, challenging sounding board. When I was CEO of Nokia India, we formed an advisory board and had experienced people such as K.V. Kamath and Balaraman V. as members. The advisory board met three to four times a year, and one of these meetings would be held at the Nokia headquarters, Helsinki. Nokia India got good value from its advisory board. At the height of the dual sim miss, I remember K.V. Kamath telling the Nokia senior leadership team in Helsinki, 'Any Indian team will get this done in a few months, don't drag your feet.' The advisory board must be owned by not just the CEO but also a few senior leadership members, else it will not work. The value comes when you treat it like a formal board with proper meetings and minutes, and not like a 'let's catch up over tea' session.

10. Good boards have a solid board evaluation process and that's a good way to give and get feedback from peers. I have seen boards get better as a result of having formal board appraisal.

Let's look at other aspects of being a board member and hear what some very qualified people in such positions have to say.

Rama Bijapurkar, a veteran on many a board, calls board membership 'jury duty'. Yale's Jeffrey Sonnenfeld says that if a board is to truly fulfil its mission, its members need to know how to 'ferret out the truth, challenge one another, and even have a good fight now and then'. The comparisons underline how critical corporate boards are for governance—to monitor performance, advise the management and provide connections. Celebrity consultant Ram Charan said, 'A board can be a competitive advantage or disadvantage, depending on the way they play their role.' As a senior manager, joining a board is a chance to showcase your skills, to learn and move to the next capability level. We live in a time when Indian industry has seen serious corporate governance failures— IL&FS, Jet Airways, Yes Bank, to name a few. Is it a good idea to join a company board, especially as an independent director?

It goes without saying that it's important to research the company, other board members, governance levels, and any underlying issues before joining one. Boards themselves need to look beyond the quarterly numbers and ask questions on the long-term strategy of the company, and sometimes about the core of the company purpose and direction. Strategy in today's VUCA (volatility, uncertainty, complexity and ambiguity) world is too risky and complex to be ignored. At the same time, governance controls through data analytics, AI, robotic process automation (RPA), blockchain and machine learning (ML) are being worked out. Reports say blockchain accounting systems will significantly reduce the need for traditional auditing.

Reshaping a Board and Its Thinking

Over the years, many remedies have been proposed to check governance lapses. From rules to procedures, composition of boards, their size and number of meetings, there are plenty of checkboxes to create vigilant boards. They don't always work. It's different with each setup as you examine the failures over the years, both in India and overseas. Take, for instance, the average age of the board. Some believe that companies would benefit from the infusion of fresh talent and insight into their boards, while others give weightage to experience. There's no denying, though, that more often than not in India, board positions go to people who are already serving on other boards. The total number of directors in India is well below the number of listed companies. The average age of directors in the NSE (National Stock Exchange) is fifty-eight, with corporate executives and retired bureaucrats having the highest presence. In a technology-led world, that average age must come down, sooner or later, into the forties. I predict that we will see many younger boards this decade. This is needed for the board and the company to feel the heat of technology disruption.

Every board has a committee to evaluate future members, as board members retire by rotation.

A survey of Indian boards by Hunt Partners found that 12 per cent of Indian companies had directors related to the promoter and 25 per cent of the companies surveyed had directors directly or indirectly related to the CEO or chairperson of the company. Both relationships can be a boardroom challenge. According to survey participants, the top three parameters that can enhance overall governance are: separating the offices of the CEO/MD and chairperson (28 per cent), mandatory formal whistle-blower policy in companies (18 per cent) and managing risks facing business (15 per cent).

Another parameter that often gets added in this discussion is the need for regular meetings. As per SEBI guidelines, an independent director can sit on the boards of not more than seven listed companies at a time. The survey found that, on an average, a director spent less than nine days on his company board in an entire year. The numbers may have changed since the survey, but even back then, this was something that

> Companies on NSE: 1818

> Individuals on the boards of NSE companies: 11,226

> Independent directors on NSE companies: 5242

> 188 individuals hold five or more than five directorships. Four hold more than eight directorships

> Only 16.87 per cent or 2543 directors are women

> Of the 1818 NSE companies, 1743 have at least one woman on the board

Source: NSE Infobase

82 per cent of the independent directors found inadequate. 'This compares very unfavourably with research results by McKinsey that identified the average work commitment in top international companies at forty days!' Damodaran suggests 16–20 days of quality time for each company. Very few board members come prepared for meetings by reading through the board deck.

Building Trust at Every Level

What makes boards great can be viewed through various lenses. Feeling trapped in the middle of regulators, shareholders, management and now the risk of regulatory action, independent directors are quitting or declining director roles in the country. This despite their remuneration having moved up over the years. The Rs 1 crore-plus club of independent directors rose over four times to eighty-nine in FY19 from twenty-one in FY13, according to Prime Database. The compensation was between Rs 1 crore to Rs 5 crore.

Remuneration alone doesn't guarantee continuity. Director compensation will be a debated question for years. Still, Nifty 500 companies saw 316 exits by independent directors in FY19, 31.7 per cent more than a year earlier, says Prime Database. Of these, ninety-nine left after their term expired. Others cited preoccupation (fifty-four), personal reasons (thirty-one) and health (ten) for leaving. About fifty quit without giving any reason. Separate figures by AIM Corporate Services LLP, a boutique forensic firm, show that 2000 independent directors quit in 2018–19. Seldom are reasons given for these exits, especially the flagging of governance standards, but there are a few exceptions. Both these firms attribute the exits to Indian laws and heavy personal liabilities. Board members who quit because they are uncomfortable with current governance rarely speak out for fear that other firms might think of them as 'troublesome board directors'.

While it's the responsibility of the board to insist it gets adequate information, Sonnenfeld says that the degree to which this doesn't happen is astonishing. According to the Hunt Partners' report, just 40 per cent of the surveyed independent directors sourced additional information to make unbiased and accurate decisions. Portea Medical CEO Meena Ganesh, who is part of a number of corporate boards, says:

> One of the reasons you join is that you feel confident about the governance of the organization. But you have to ask questions regarding any decision taken. Even if you are not a part of certain committees, normally somebody always reports to the board about dealings and findings or certain outcomes, so you have to keep your ears open for any red flags regarding the company, both internally and from the market.

Only 8 per cent of the companies in India had a lead independent director, who primarily reviewed and advised the board on agenda and represented the views of the other independent directors. About 35 per cent of the companies had the agenda authored by independent directors, thereby undermining their participation and contribution in these meetings. So, some changes are needed in the ways of working.

Women on the Board

When it comes to board composition, studies have shown that having women on the board results in better decisions and significantly better results. 'One benefit of having female directors on the board is a greater diversity of viewpoints, which is purported to improve the quality of board deliberations, especially when complex issues are involved, because different perspectives can increase the amount of information available,' says *Harvard Business Review*.

WOMEN ON BOARDS - HISTORICAL TABLE

Source: Prime Database

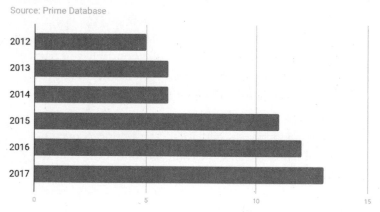

European nations took the lead here by adopting regulatory quotas for women's representation. Norway was one of the first countries to set a benchmark. In 2003, the Norwegian government passed a law that required companies to have at least 40 per cent of board members to be women. India enforced a quota to have at least one woman director on the board in 2013. Consequently, after coming into force in 2014, the numbers have gone up. Female representation in the Nifty 500, which was at 5 per cent as on 31 March 2012, increased to 13 per cent as on 31 March 2017, inching up to 15 per cent in 2019. Women are still underrepresented in stewardship roles, though, lower than countries such as Norway (39 per cent), France (34 per cent), the UK (23 per cent) and the USA (21 per cent). However, the silly notion that women directors only get appointed from promoter families to comply with regulations is not true. A large proportion of women are independent directors, but most firms have not cared to go beyond the mandated requirement. Sixty per cent of the Nifty 500 firms had just that one woman on board that the law mandates as of FY2019. A *Mint* report shows that 31 per cent had two

WOMEN DIRECTORS BY COMPANY OWNERSHIP

Source: Prime Database

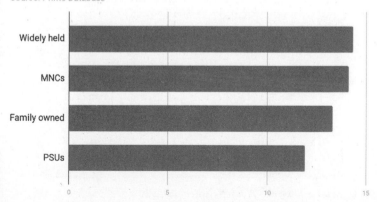

women on their boards and 5 per cent had three. Only eleven companies, or 2.2 per cent of the Nifty 500 firms, had more than three women on their board.

Companies may want to remedy that. 'Research has found that female directors tend to be less conformist and more likely to express their independent views than male directors as they do not belong to the old-boy network. So, a board with women directors might be more likely to challenge the CEO and push him to consider a wider range of options, as well as pros and cons, when making strategic decisions,' adds *Harvard Business Review*.

Reading the Fine Print

Even a single dissenter can make a huge difference on a board. It is the ability to ask the right questions that can save a company. CEOs who don't welcome dissent try to

> 1630 companies listed on NSE

> 1344 companies that saw independent directors quitting during FY2020

> Of these, 296 directors cited personal reasons

> 184 directors retired or their term ended and did not offer themselves for reappointment

Source: *Economic Times*, 9 September 2020

pack the board, which can turn out to be disastrous. There are several ways in which things could go awry. Sometimes, if a board member challenges a major decision, a company can go to great lengths to discredit the person. Political factions may develop on the board due to lack of trust from management, which sees the board as an 'obstacle to be managed'. It could be that board members are excessively political and pursuing agendas they don't want the CEO to know about. It all comes down to evaluating the management beforehand.

R.R. Nair, with his wide experience, lays out some important questions one should ask before committing to a board:

> Do they have strong internal control systems, time-tested and adaptive to changing situations? Are they fair in their dealings with employees? Do they adhere to the highest norms of conduct, values and behaviours while dealing with investors, financial institutions, regulatory authorities and other key stakeholders? What is the quality of the executive management? Does the organization value meritocracy? Do they have a planned career planning and succession management process? Does the organization strive to become future-ready in order to deal with the complexities of the environment in which the business is operating?

These questions can act as a guide to scrutinize governance levels. At the end of the day, joining a board is about what you can bring to the table and take away from it. A board,

Balaraman V. says, should have a mix of people—some who understand strategy, some who understand law and some who understand the industry. One needs to analyse how one's expertise fits in and what's the learning to be gained. For Meena Ganesh, a different industry opens avenues to more learning. Being on diverse boards can truly help expand your own horizon, but only if you are ready for 'jury duty'.

Balaraman V., founder, Boardroom Advantage

Balaraman V. is founder, Boardroom Advantage, a company that offers brand marketing consultancy, coaching and mentoring to current and potential leaders. He has been a career Unilever man, joining the company after finishing his MBA from IIM Ahmedabad in 1970. At Unilever, Balaraman straddled many roles, including MD and CEO, Pond's India, and director, exports, HUL. He then became MD and CEO, Adrenalin E Systems Ltd., a Polaris Group company, between 2002 and 2006. He currently serves as a non-executive director on the boards of numerous companies. In the past, he has also served as president of the Madras Chamber of Commerce and Industry, Madras Management Association, Indian Shoe Federation, Federation of Indian Export Organizations Southern Region, and chairman of the Footwear Design and Development Institute.

You have been part of many committees that choose board members. What qualities do you look for in members?

I look at whether the board member will be able to add value by bringing in a new perspective. On a board, each member should have a perspective and should be able to speak up. It depends on the slot domain we have open in every board. In one company, if you are looking for industry experience, in another company, you are looking for legal expertise. So, multiple purposes are looked at.

So, you look for multiple skill sets in order to have a board that is equipped to handle different domains of knowledge?

Yes. I would also say that board members should have the ability to add value. Every director must add a new strength that the board does not have. A board should be able to do many things. It should have some people who understand strategy, some who understand law, and some who understand the industry.

You are on multiple boards yourself. What criteria do you use to pick board memberships?

I look at whether there is an opportunity to contribute, if I can make any difference to the board. I also see if the company is ethical and principled, and if it really needs me.

Kirthiga Reddy, partner, SoftBank Investment Advisers, and former managing director, Facebook India and South Asia

You are on a few boards. A dilemma people have is how to choose a board role. What factors do you consider when you pick a board role?

I look at three fundamental factors for anything I do, including board roles: Is it a bold mission that I believe in? Are there people I can learn from? Do I bring expertise to be a game changer towards the mission?

This framework helps with next-level questions. Public vs private board? Academic board or, more broadly, non-profit board? Is it in an industry where you bring domain expertise? Or outside the industry of expertise, where you bring your functional skills? What board culture would you thrive in? The answers are very individual. To be complete in the assessment criteria, be aware of the liabilities associated with being on the board.

Once on a board, invest in the onboarding phase. If this is your first board, learn about the role and responsibilities of being a board member. If it's a new industry, learn about the industry. Invest in relationships with the executive team and the rest of the board. Understand key near- and long-term strategic decisions. Understand the difference between accountability as an operating executive vs the guidance and governance responsibility as a board member. Finally, if not already a practice, be sure to advocate for annual board assessments!

M. Damodaran, chairperson, Excellence Enablers and former chairman, SEBI, UTI and IDBI

Meleveetil Damodaran is one of the most sought-after independent directors in India and has been on the boards of several blue-chip companies such as Larsen & Toubro, Hero MotoCorp, Tech Mahindra, CRISIL, Biocon and Experian India. He is founder chairperson, Excellence Enablers Private Limited, a niche corporate governance advisory firm, and founder and managing trustee, Non-Executive Directors in Conversation Trust (NEDICT), an exclusive forum for non-executive directors. He has had an illustrious career as a senior government official and has served as chairman of several organizations, such as SEBI, UTI and IDBI. He was appointed chairman of IndiGo (InterGlobe Aviation) on 24 January 2019.

How does a senior manager evaluate a board role that comes their way? What variables should one think of?

Just as a company evaluates a potential candidate for appointment as a director, every potential director should undertake due diligence of the company concerned. In particular, this due diligence should address the financial performance of the company, the quality of the board of directors, the regulatory track record of the company, and concerns, if any, flagged by the auditors. The annual report of the company, particularly the chapters on corporate governance and management discussion and analysis, are indicative of the general standing of the company.

On an average, how much time should one be able to dedicate to their board duty/company?

It is not enough for directors to satisfy themselves with attending board meetings. Every independent director joining the board should be prepared to serve on at least two committees. With many companies having more than the statutorily prescribed four board meetings, and with committee meetings being at least as many as board meetings, a director should set apart ten to fifteen days for such meetings. This does not include the time commitment for going through the board and committee agenda papers before the meetings. In addition, it is useful for directors to interact in a planned manner with senior management personnel, between the board meeting dates. Taking all of this into account, the director would be expected to commit sixteen to twenty days of quality time for each company on whose board/committees he/she sits.

There is a tendency to take on as many board roles as possible after retirement. How many boards can a board member truly do justice to, and why?

The tendency to take on a large number of board positions, especially after retirement, is, at one level, indicative of the inadequate compensation given to independent directors. Considering the time for board and committee meetings, and with the requisite extent of meaningful involvement, a director cannot do justice to more than four boards. Even this is premised on the understanding that he/she does not have a regular day job.

What advice would you have for first-time board members? How should they approach this role and how should a company onboarding them prepare the new entrants?

Before a board member attends his/her first meeting, it is necessary to subject that person to an immersion programme comprising one-on-one interactions with senior management personnel including, but not limited to, key managerial personnel. This is necessary so that, during the first meeting, the new member does not look entirely out of place in the boardroom. In addition, with the increasing use of abbreviations in board agenda papers as well as in boardroom conversations, it is necessary to obtain a list of abbreviations that are being used, with their expansions and, where necessary, their meanings.

From your vantage point, what are the characteristics of a good board?

A good board, in addition to being one with diversity not merely with regard to gender but also of age, experience and geography, should be a cohesive board in search of solutions. It should not degenerate into a debating club where everyone has a say but no clear conclusion emerges. More importantly, the board should be able to constructively challenge the management on a continuing basis.

How should a board member handle disagreement with other board members, with the chairman, and with other operating executives?

Disagreements, if any, should be minimal. Initial attempts to address disagreements should take place outside the boardrooms. Often, disagreement arises from asymmetry of information. Wherever there are differences in approach or in regard to the desirability of a proposal, there should be active discussions in the boardroom. Where a director is convinced that he/she is not in agreement with the views of the majority, a dissenting opinion may be recorded after attempts to find agreement do not succeed. Dissent is the last option and should not be resorted to very frequently.

Is it necessary for board members to have some subject matter expertise so as to be clued in to the conversation in a meeting? Many members look at this role as a fiduciary duty and ignore this aspect. Is that worrying?

It is not necessary for members to have subject matter expertise. Domain awareness and domain knowledge are positive attributes, but domain expertise can sometimes be counterproductive if it results in second guessing the management on a continuing basis.

Rama Bijapurkar, independent director and thought leader

Rama Bijapurkar is a thought leader on market strategy and India's consumer economy. She works across sectors and organizations and describes her mission as 'bringing market and customer focus to business strategy'. Bijapurkar has served as an independent director on the boards of several of India's blue-chip companies including Axis Bank, Bharat Petroleum, CRISIL, Godrej Consumer Products, Infosys, ICICI Prudential Life Insurance, Mahindra & Mahindra Financial Services Ltd, and Redington Gulf FZE. She also serves on the governing councils of the Banking Codes and Standards Board of India, and the Insurance Information Board, and is a member of the Eminent Persons Advisory Group of the Competition Commission of India. She is also visiting faculty at IIM Ahmedabad, her alma mater, and is a member of its board of governors.

How does one go about choosing a board role?

I want to point out that the biggest dilemma is when to quit, not what to join. That is a much simpler thing, to be honest. But when to quit is a big dilemma, because there are a whole host of factors—ethical, moral, legal, institutional. It's a whole mess.

If you do a day job spectacularly, companies will come and find you wherever you are. You will then get offers to come on to the boards to take up the fiduciary responsibilities of supervising a company. So, you make choices, but you don't prepare to join a board. The first serious board I was invited on was Infosys because I was a fit. The last one I went on was ICICI because the institution was in trouble and they wanted plain speak, so they chose me.

What parameters did you use to say yes or no to board roles?

If the company is dodgy, you don't go on it. Boards are essentially very simple; they have been mystified. So, if it is a Rana Kapoor board, don't go on it, because everyone is talking about their issues. If it is an ICICI Bank board, have a straight chat with the chairman and ask them if they have done any deals that you don't know about. So, one part of it is the elimination. And another part is to see who else is on the board. Are they people you respect? Are their values in consonance with yours? If not, then don't do it, no matter how much the money is. Essentially, the choice is about the price you are willing to pay, and what you are willing to take for what you get. So, it's a very simple framework.

Are you willing to transgress on your value system and put your reputation at risk for money and bonuses?

Choices are a function of what you want and what's on offer. It is at the intersection of the two that you make one. So, at one point in life, I might decide that I really want to see a lot of hard-core businesses and want to do a deep dive into India Inc. as it is evolving, in which case you will pick one company of each kind. Sometimes you might do it because once a quarter you want to get lectured to, so it's a really good knowledge bucket, in addition to all the other things. At one point I was on a board that showed me a lot of rural India; at another, I was on a board that was of interest to me from a micro-consumer point of view. I've been on banking boards, on the board of a credit rating agency, etc. So, there is a combination of things.

What makes an effective board member?

I've said this repeatedly. What you need to do as a board member is jury duty. And there are three or four other things as well. One is jury duty, where you are being paid for your judgement. The board of directors is not a board of consultants. Obviously, when we talk about diversity on a board, each of us is wired in a way that's defined by our experiences and our personal areas of expertise. So, clearly, a lawyer will think differently from a marketing person, who will think differently from a banker or a CEO. But one of the parameters of a board function is the ability to participate on issues outside your narrow little silo. So, whenever a board comes to me that sounds like a BOC (board of consultants) rather than a BOD (board of directors), I say no to it. Because that's cheap consulting and not fiduciary responsibility towards the company. A lot of promoter boards say, 'We love your marketing advice, why don't you come on our board?' I wonder why they don't hire a marketing consultant.

What, in your experience, is the difference between an operating manager being a board member and a retired manager being a board member?

The role of a board, as I've written extensively, is nose in and fingers out. So, if you are capable of putting your nose in and fingers out, go on a board, but if your fingers are itching to get in, then don't. For the operating guys, it's much harder because you have to ask free questions about why the operations are the way they are and not go in there and say, 'I'll tell you what to do.'

You cannot be at the buy side and the sell side. You cannot be cosying up with the CEO and the management and the HR, telling them how to run their factory, and then sit in judgement and approve their expenditure. Your colleagues will also go hands off if they find out that you've done a deep dive with the management. So, let's be absolutely clear on the role of the board—it is jury duty, it is to make sure there is no value destruction, to make sure that there is a long line of succession so that if someone screws up, they can be replaced without the company missing a beat. It is to ensure that honesty and integrity towards stakeholders is maintained.

Debjani Ghosh, president, NASSCOM

You are on a few boards. What factors do you consider when joining a board, either advisory or a listed entity?

I have actually not been on any company boards since I joined NASSCOM to avoid any conflict of interest. However, the advice I always give to anyone who is interested in joining a board is to do very thorough diligence on understanding the role of the board. Is the board really contributing as a board should and is the company leveraging the board to the fullest vs using it as a showpiece? I am obsessed with ethics, and it's very important for me to fully understand the governance practices the company has in place before considering a board position. And, when looking at governance, it's important to see not just what they do, but what they don't do because of their guardrails. Are they going walk from a business opportunity if it poses ethical challenges? It is also important to look at who the other members are and what their experience has been so far. Last but not the least, I always worry when boards are too aligned and always in agreement. There has to be a healthy culture of questioning and dissonance for a board to add real value.

Five Things to Remember about This Dilemma

1. Independent directors are quitting or refusing a seat on the board because of the risk of regulatory action.
2. More women on the board can enhance strategic decision making.
3. Having directors related to promoters, the CEO or the chairman is a boardroom challenge.
4. Getting onto a board will enhance your personal network.
5. Boards need to get younger.

Dilemma 10

Dilemma of a CEO

The CEO job is an aspirational one, and the outside view is that it is an easy job where you tell people what to do and then it gets done. Nothing is farther from the truth. Many people think that once you are a CEO, you have arrived and can take it easy. In fact, the challenge starts when you become a CEO. Nothing prepares you for being a CEO, not even the number of GM roles you have done before.

The CEO's Take

In August 2020, I asked about twenty leaders about their biggest dilemma in a normal year running their company. Here is a list of things that they regarded as their biggest dilemma:

1. Piyush Pandey, chairman, Ogilvy: 'I normally don't worry too much. I only think of how best I can look after my team. They make us win. There is no dilemma on that. If I have a great team, business will grow.'

2. Suresh Narayanan, chairman and MD, Nestlé India: 'My biggest dilemma is whether we grow faster top line or grow stronger in terms of margins, and which is the better approach for our stakeholders?'

3. Satish Pai, MD, Hindalco: 'How to meet the sustainability expectations of the various stakeholders is the biggest dilemma.'

4. Vanitha Narayanan, ex-CEO, IBM India: 'My dilemma was instilling a sense of urgency with a systematic approach. Execution was more frantic than urgent, and often, it was a case of heroics versus systemic orchestration.'

5. Ashish Dikshit, CEO, ABFRL (Aditya Birla Fashion and Retail): 'The biggest dilemma is around capital allocation—human and financial. Do we invest behind new categories or build existing ones? The first is cheaper and less risky and gets good returns but doesn't build new muscles, and hence no play in new segments with new customers.'

6. Dilip Gaur, MD, Grasim: 'Managing trade-offs is the biggest dilemma, managing short term versus long term, strategic versus tactical, potential versus performance, etc. There are no thumb rules or benchmarks here. A CEO has to have a self-optimizing algorithm as we see in machine learning.'

7. Renuka Ramnath, founder and CEO, Multiples Alternate Asset Management: 'My dilemma has been whether I should take quick action on a non-performer or someone I don't fully trust, or prepare the organization and other stakeholders before I take the call. I might have stretched it in a few cases.'

8. An MNC CEO who didn't want to be quoted: 'My biggest dilemma is to manage unrealistic expectations of global HQ. The pressure to act bold and entrepreneurial and yet play safe and deliver despite slow ways of working in the company.'

9. Vineet Taneja, CEO, Dyson Asia: 'My biggest dilemma is how to build a talent pool that can deliver today and can be future-ready at the same time.'

10. Vipul Sabharwal, CEO, Luminous: 'My biggest dilemma is whether we are investing enough in the future and technology.'

11. Avani Davda, ex-CEO, Starbucks India: 'My dilemma has been to get focus on long-term investment in a phase of steady consolidating competition.'

12. V. Ramnath, ex-CEO, Racold: 'My biggest dilemma as a CEO is to manage the pace of change required to take the organization forward.'

13. Prakash Nedungadi, ex-CEO, Aditya Birla Fashion: 'My biggest dilemma is deploying time between long-term needs and short-term compulsions.'

14. Madhusudan Gopalan, CEO, P&G India: 'My biggest dilemma is balancing short-term target delivery with mid/long-term interventions that are right for the business/organization.'

15. Ajey Mehta, ex-CEO, Nokia India: 'My biggest dilemma was choosing between scale and profit.'

16. Simeen Hossein, CEO, Transcom Bangladesh: 'My biggest dilemma is bringing in fresh capable talent versus continuing with those who have been loyal to the company throughout their career but have plateaued.

Manoeuvring this without disrupting the company and its culture is a big dilemma.'

17. R.S. Subramanian, MD, DHL India: 'My biggest dilemma is the classic one—volume growth versus yield, cost versus quality and short-term goals versus long-term needs. Invariably, a CEO has to take the short-term hits in favour of the long term; vote for quality, and hold your yield.'

18. Shashi Sinha, CEO, Lodestar: 'My biggest dilemma is recruiting and retaining quality talent.'

19. Devendra Chawla, CEO, RPG Retail: 'My biggest dilemma is managing the challenge of setting team targets and aligning them versus the actuals, which then happen as a result of each team member looking at them mentally and emotionally from their goals perspective. This variable delivery despite common alignment is a dilemma.'

20. Hema Hattangadi, CEO, Conzerv Systems: 'When business was booming, the dilemma was IPR (intellectual property rights) theft by a long-term R&D employee. Otherwise, it is always about conserving cash without affecting morale and losing customers.'

One can see that there is a wide range of dilemmas which top the list for a CEO. This obviously means that the context of the company and industry matters, the competitive position of the company matters, the stakeholders matter and the years a CEO has spent in the role matter!

My Take

While the business realities are what they are, each CEO has his/her own way of identifying and addressing them.

The dilemmas relate to the softer side of how you do the job. I am listing a few of them here (not a complete list) based on my observations of CEOs.

The First Ninety Days

When I became a CEO, the following five things in the first ninety days surprised me:

1. The day never seemed to end. The calendar stayed full, day in and day out. This led to two challenges—one was the ability to maintain energy through the day and the second was to find some 'me time', or personal space, for reflection. It is easy to become a slave to the job with loads of activity as opposed to thinking about the future and resetting the agenda. Without time for reflection, a CEO will become an efficiency engine and not a value-creating leader.

2. Everyone wants you in on the information loop. Every email is marked to you, every note is sent to you. There are so many issues which people believe have reputational risks and hence need your attention. The challenge is to stay away from the decision loop even as information keeps gathering momentum. The information tells you how the company is working, who gets along, who is adversarial, and so on. The key is to absorb rather than adjudicate early.

3. Managing the stakeholders—the parent company, your own subordinates, the media, the board, the ecosystem partners. Everyone wants to get a sense of you and do a quick tea/coffee meeting, and finding that time is near

impossible. I think one needs to prioritize the important engagements and deal with them quickly.

4. The apostle of the company culture: When you become the CEO, your words and actions set the tone from the top. Sometimes the tone can be positive, and at other times it can leave the wrong impression. Everything you do in the first ninety days will be watched minutely and dissected threadbare for positives and negatives. You will have an equal number of admirers and detractors. People mimic both good and bad bosses, they start using your expressions, mimic the way you conduct meetings and so on. A good way to think about this is to stay neutral in the first three months and absorb as much you can, before you try and shift direction.

5. The fifth and final thing that surprised me was to judge who will tell you the truth and who will tell you what they think you want to hear. Most people don't want to get on the wrong side of a CEO by telling him the harsh truth. I always valued people who told me the blunt truth and then I could get on and deal with it. I categorized people thus: those who told me the truth in the best hope that I would do something about it; those who told me a positive version of the truth so that they looked good and they thought they were protecting me; those who told me the truth but were cynical about it, saying things like 'Nothing will change, you will realize this soon enough'; and those who would never tell me the truth. A CEO forms and develops trust based on which type of person he starts valuing.

Typical Dilemmas

Moving on from the first ninety days, given below are some aspects that CEOs should think about:

1. What kind of legacy do you want to leave as CEO?

CEOs have a shelf life, and their average tenure is dropping. In the UK, the average tenure of a CEO in 2010 was 8.3 years; in 2019, that had dropped to 4.6 years, nearly half the tenure in just a decade. The Equilar Strategy study of 2017 found that the S&P 500 list CEOs had tenures of five years.

The CEO job, in the best of times, is a tough and lonely one where you get more brickbats than bouquets. *What do I want to leave behind, what do I want to be remembered for?* This is a question on every CEO's mind. Nearly half the CEOs polled by a leading magazine want to be remembered for growth and for transforming the business. In the past, most of the legacy discussion was around business results; of late, we are seeing that personal qualities are becoming important in the legacy question and nearly a third of CEOs list them on their legacy sheet. The personal qualities that add to legacy are: integrity, honesty, ethical leadership, transparency and fairness.

The results and the efforts are visible to all. Luck plays an important role in results, apart from strategy and execution. Every performance can be appreciated or criticized based on the lens you use. CEOs rarely get credit for fundamental turnaround these days because people rarely have the ability to take a long view, and also because it means one has to accept that the past was flawed.

The dilemma most CEOs go through is a choice between being popular or liked versus being respected. Every CEO will have his set of supporters and detractors. So, trying to be popular is a futile exercise since you can never please everyone. In my experience, the best CEOs first do what's right for the company, then for the team and lastly for themselves. When CEOs start looking after their own interests first, the company gets in trouble. I have seen, at close quarters, personal ambitions of a few leaders destroy the fabric of a company that was once great.

Is time a factor in legacy? In today's times, when the tenure is short, it really doesn't play a role. This means that you have to hit the ground running from day one of the job.

Is the performance of the company after a CEO's departure a factor? I think if the CEO has spent more than ten years, it would certainly be a factor. However, with swift market changes, the new CEO has to do his thing.

2. What type of a CEO job is worth it and how should one think about it?

There are various types of CEO roles and while the designation is common, the company, its history, its immediate results and employee morale are things to think about.

Here are some points to consider before taking the plunge:

The first is what I label a 'no-win job'.

There are some jobs which are in the no-win bracket or the definition of success is set very high. Let's take sports as an analogy.

The captain of the Indian cricket team, the country football manager's job in Brazil and Argentina, the manager's job at Manchester United and Barcelona football clubs—these are all no-win jobs. The bar is high and the stakeholders expect nothing but the winner's trophy. A runner-up trophy is not a consolation.

Picking this type of a job has little upside and a lot of downside.

The second is to think of whom you are succeeding.

Taking over from someone who has spent significant time on the job is a challenge in itself. You have to come out of that shadow and establish yourself. There are good and bad examples of this. Immelt followed Jack Welch at GE (General Electric) and the jury is not kind to Immelt; Tim Cook followed Steve Jobs at Apple and has succeeded; K.V. Kamath took over from Vaghul at ICICI and did very well; Balaraman V. took over from V. Narayanan at Pond's India and took the company to new heights.

When you are in this situation, it is important to recognize that there is a certain habit or way of working that the company has become used to. Hence, breaking or moving away from that takes time and will come with resistance. However, you have to be your person and do what's right.

The third issue is whether your predecessor continues in the system.

This is another difficult situation and I've encountered it. It is unlikely that your predecessor will be happy with what you want to change because it is an indictment of his thinking and strategic skills. The way to deal with it is to do what's best for the organization, hope that people in the system will see your genuineness and not worry about the insecurities of your predecessor.

In my case, this predecessor would keep calling some people whom he saw as his confidants to try and get updates. It was childish behaviour on his part and I never bothered about it. It was a nuisance and an embarrassment for the people he called. He came from an advertising background and never really understood either execution or strategy.

When I handed over to Balaji in Nokia and I was still in the system, I ensured that he had a free hand and did what he thought right. My job was to open doors and ensure that his voice was heard. I stepped in only when he asked for help.

The fourth issue is whether you have a say in who your successor is.

Whom you hand over to is also an important ingredient of your legacy. In some companies, especially at senior levels, the incumbent CEO might have a say in who his successor will be. Many CEOs or division heads try to game the system and pick someone who is close to them and who will make them look good after they leave. When this happens, the organization is always slow to get back to being competitive. The new CEO cannot challenge what his predecessor did since he owes his job to that person. That lack of objectivity hurts the company.

The fifth issue is the time horizon of the job.

Most organizations want growth and business transformation in today's environment when they give you the CEO's job. You have to be clear that transformation is possible in the time frame you have in mind. Some turnarounds take longer, and people might not be able to see the deep problems facing the company when they give you the job.

When I started at Nokia, I had the benefit of a strong brand and good growth. I gave myself five years, but ended up spending more than five years. When I took over at PepsiCo, I faced all the challenges I have listed here. Once again, I gave myself five years but moved on in four years.

The time horizon depends on whether the company backs your strategy and is willing to see it through. There are companies where strategy changes with the whims and fancies of a few HQ people; that kind of company is a lose-lose for you. You can never win when there is constant changing or 'whimsical strategy'.

The sixth and final point is what to do after this job.

If you get a CEO break in your mid-fifties, then you would likely retire and serve on a few boards and drive into the sunset. This is an easy situation and does not pose a dilemma.

If you are a young CEO in your forties, then you have this question to ponder. After your CEO stint you might not want to go to another company in the same industry, as you will be seen as a mercenary and lose a lot of your personal credibility. So, you might have to look at other industries and thus enhance your longevity while giving yourself the space to learn fresh skills.

There is a study that shows that people have the maximum energy in their twenties, the maximum wisdom a little after sixty, and the ideal combination of energy and wisdom in their early forties.

3.   Relationship with bosses

A CEO too has a boss. In the case of an MNC CEO, it can be a regional person, an HQ person; in the case of a listed entity, it can be the chairman of the board, the leader of the conglomerate and the board. Whoever your boss may be, you have to think about how you work with that person.

I don't think any CEO starts off by wanting to have anything but a productive relationship with his/her boss.

At senior levels, I feel people have to work as equals and colleagues, and not follow the line of a reporting relationship. Senior-level relationships are built on respect, and hierarchy doesn't build respect. Many bosses expect excessive fawning and attention and Indian managers are perceived as doing more of it. However, I must add that I have seen this fawning behaviour in all cultures. I have seen that when the stakes are high for senior managers, they tend to pander to their boss so much more.

I have always seen it in terms of first respecting the individual for his/her capabilities, and then checking the person's character consistency in the way he/she works. In many cases, it's the second part where your boss will fall short. You would be plain unlucky if you get an incompetent boss who is also whimsical.

Disagreements with bosses will always be there, and if the relationship is healthy, the disagreements will also be healthy and issue-based. In my experience, disagreements typically centre on the scope of ambition at the time of the annual plan, the issue of judging talent in people, media messaging, and a view of future developments.

What's difficult for a talented CEO is to have a boss who is incompetent, insecure and obsesses over detail. A boss like this adds zero value; you are constantly thinking of avoiding this guy at all costs. I had one such boss in my career. He would keep sending emails every day; one-hour meetings with him would produce more slogans such as 'Let's power ahead', and the team would end up with thirty more action points, all of which he would stupidly want updates on, every week. He was an intellectually dishonest guy and people had zero respect for him.

What's the best way to work towards a productive relationship with the boss?

I can quote what worked for me with every boss:

a. Holding a monthly meeting where I would send the boss a one-pager on what I would cover and then briefing him/her on key issues and progress in the business.
b. I would always send notes of my travel and customer meetings to both my boss and my team. This ensured that we were all on the same page.
c. I would disagree when I felt the need to and I could accept a challenge anytime, but I just couldn't handle intellectual

dishonesty. Sometimes, the boss tries to convince you that we must do something because it's good for the company and you know that it's dead wrong—those are moments to watch out for.

d. Most bosses expect no surprises, and one should try and avoid a surprise. However, the definition of a surprise itself can vary between competent and incompetent bosses. You have to judge that.

4. Managing and working with the media

Managing media relations is an important CEO role. A University of San Diego School of Journalism study of thirty-six CEOs of the Top 100 Fortune companies shows what we have known all along: 'There is a positive correlation between CEO visibility and organization visibility. The CEO tone sets the tone for organizational tone.'

Every organization wants a good reputation. Warren Buffett said in 2010: 'We can afford to lose money, even a lot of money, but we cannot lose our reputation, even a shred of reputation.'

The size of a company has nothing to do with media engagement or which CEOs the media wants to talk to. It's more the thought leadership of the CEO and his/her ability to give a balanced picture to the media. In most countries, the media have a set of CEOs they speak with.

There are many benefits of CEO presence in the media. They can clarify strategy and company approach; they can calm the media when hot issues surface. The latter are not there only to portray the CEO and the company in a positive light.

I believe that the media is neither friend nor foe. It has a role to perform and will do what in its view is right for its readers or viewers. I have seen some CEOs go overboard in cultivating media houses, feeding them tips from time to time. I have also seen CEOs freeze and become very uncomfortable dealing with the media. The mistake CEOs make is to think that the media will print the briefing document in full or portray the CEO view only, after a thirty-minute interview. CEOs are shocked to see just one line or quote in the newspaper appear afterwards. Nothing can shatter a CEO's ego more.

I remember when the Nokia BL 5C battery recall happened, I spoke with A.P. Parigi, director of Bennett Coleman, the late Parthasarathi Swamy, editor at *Business World* and T.K. Arun at the *Economic Times* for advice. They were clear and very helpful in how I should manage the media crisis that followed. That's the only time I was on Arnab Goswami's show (then with *Times Now*).

We had many media challenges when I was CEO. We had the battery crisis, the radiation crisis, the dual sim crisis, the Windows failed strategy crisis, the crisis around KKR's IPL (Indian Premier League) performance in the first three seasons and the IPL sponsorship in the betting-scandal era. In each of these, we prepared well and gave the media a balanced picture of the situation.

For most of my CEO career, I overlapped with Poonam Kaul, one of the best communications specialists as my communications director. She had annual media off-sites where the management team got to know the media, and their coverage wasn't just about the CEO but every management team member. This gave the company a broader appeal and we could also choose who would speak and on what topic. Many companies tend to have only their CEO and CFO speak to the media; I feel that's a narrow strategy. I would encourage even marketing heads to engage with the media. This ensures that the media sees many more people and gets a more balanced picture.

Having the CEO manage the media also helps in attracting talent and ecosystem partners, opening doors to government offices and building B2B relationships. One cannot assign a numerical value to this, but it's important.

Many companies want the media when they are in trouble; they are not available when the media wants them for a quote or perspective, though. That's a narrow view. One has to be friendly in good times as well as bad times. I maintain that the CEO of a company is the ambassador of the company. An ambassador cannot have a bad day; a minister can! A CEO who remembers that will do well with the media.

If you are not available to the media and don't manage them constructively, they will assess you, the CEO and the company. One can easily make out whether a CEO is being a star communicator for his company or trying to build his/her own persona. In my career, I must have had a maximum of five personal stories; every interaction of mine has been around the company and its issues, never the personal side. It has become fashionable for CEOs to talk about their houses, their holidays, their wristwatches, etc. In my view, these do not add value to the company you represent. There is another fad now—being featured on Page 3 (of *Bombay Times*). In the eyes of many employees at that time, a leading FMCG fell from its high position when the CEO of the company was seen regularly on Page 3. In the eyes of committed managers, Page 1 and Page 3 are like chalk and cheese.

The Indian media is very different from the media in other countries. Here, they ask for a lot of numbers, for guidance, challenge the opinions expressed by the CEO and talk to competitors before they come for your briefing. Everyone wants a unique byte or story, so they abhor the grand media briefing. They are happier doing one-on-one interviews. Everyone wants an 'exclusive' and a 'breaking story'.

My final learning—it's best to be your authentic self and do what's right for the company in all media interactions. I have received my share of bouquets and brickbats from the media, but on balance, I must say they were fair to me 95 per cent of the time.

5.   How much time to spend on growing future leaders?

Every company has a plan to grow future leaders and this is an area where the CEO can leave a strong impact.

The HR department has a list of potential future leaders. Grooming them and making them match fit is a responsibility which the CEO can share in. This is always a dilemma because there are managers who have been around for some time, and for the CEO to spend time with young people is a challenge of time and commitment and a matter of abandoning the trusted for the untested.

We tried a number of things to develop a wide range of future leaders.

Young people like to be connected with senior leaders. We started the shadow programme where young people could spend a week with senior managers, watching them through every meeting, every situation. This was a huge success in every company where I ran it. The shadowee saw the dilemmas involved when the CEO made decisions, and the CEO received feedback on their verbal and non-verbal behaviour through the day.

We tried a unique experiment with millennials which turned out successful—the concept of a Gen Y board. We got millennials to elect ten representatives on their own and handed over all company events to this youth board. The elections were amazingly creative and I believe the millennials felt a lot better, represented via the Gen Y board. As CEO, I would meet them every month to get an update and to clear any pathways for them to be more effective. The biggest benefit of the Gen Y board has been in the area of digital where the board came up with ideas to digitize as also to up our company digital media presence.

As CEO, I had regular roundtables with as many people in the organization as possible, with an emphasis on future leaders. I looked more for commitment to the company and its cause as the differentiating factor in my time investment. Young people are more open in such relaxed settings as opposed to formal town halls, where they worry that their voice could get drowned or frowned on.

Getting the top set of leaders is also important. At Nokia, we had the Top 30 meeting every quarter, while at PepsiCo, we had the Top 300 in a programme called 'Stay a Leader— CEO—Collaborate, Execute, Own'. The idea was to build

300 CEOs in the organization who would become apostles of the company agenda. In these sessions, I would share the progress on my targets. I did this to ensure that no one felt that the CEO was carrying easier targets. This gave people confidence in their efforts, including their discretionary ones, for the company.

At a difficult juncture in transforming PepsiCo, we started the ambassador programme, where we assembled and sieved around seventy-five leaders based on their performance and the values they displayed, not their seniority. We asked them to carry forward the narrative of the transformation. Some people who were not invited were miffed, but we had to make a distinction between true ambassadors of the company and those who paid it mere lip service.

For the CEO, the dilemma is about the time spent and the returns. The return on this initiative is not immediate, it happens over time. But when done right, it creates enormous energy in the company and helps you stay connected with this youthful energy. You are proud when you see them do well over the years.

6. Should a CEO use social media?

I have not been on social media for most of my CEO career. I got onto social media only after I joined ABG on 1 January 2018. I am on LinkedIn, but not on any other platform.

Why did I skip social media?

My long-time communications director, Poonam Kaul, specifically barred me from social media because she felt that I would reply to every message that was directed at me, creating more challenges for the communications team.

Social media is here to stay whether CEOs want to be on it or not.

A CEO being on social media makes him/her more informal, more approachable. Typical followers of your social media profile tend to be employees, ecosystem partners, media, investors, and industry peers.

A CEO who is on social media and posts cool, relevant content is seen as a forward-looking, innovative, in-touch-with-reality CEO. Only 50 per cent of CEOs are active on social media. They cite lack of time, they feel that it is for young people and they themselves have nothing to gain from it, they feel the return on investment is not clear and that it is risky. However, people see the CEO who is on social media in a positive light.

As I mentioned, I am on LinkedIn where I share summaries of books I have read (an old habit), and I also share presentations and speeches I make at various fora and platforms. People who follow me are CEOs, CXOs, salespeople and entrepreneurs.

What kind of content works with my audience?

When I just started out on LinkedIn, my friend Chandramouli Venkatesan asked me to do a video clip to promote his book *The Catalyst*. In the video clip, I proposed that one should not work for an incompetent or insecure boss, that it is better to move on from such a boss. Mouli wasn't sure how it would be received and he probably ran it reluctantly since there was no other version I had done. But it became one of the most watched and forwarded videos.

So, from this I learnt about what content works with my audience. It includes: Content that is data-rich about India and the world. Content that is about personal growth and development. Content that is emotional. Content that is forward-looking.

Being on social media is not an easy ride. I have encountered the following challenges:

A. People using my post to advertise something they are part of. I try and ensure that I block this type of person as I don't want my audience to think I would be party to any such activity.

B. People who write to me asking me to summarize their book so that it will sell better. Books are a hobby for me; I tend to summarize those that I believe will have value for my audience. I do not advertise any book. If I genuinely think that the book has meaningful insights, I post about it. Professor Jagdish Sheth, Rama Bijapurkar and Piyush Pandey have got back to me stating that my summary of their book was good and they would use my slides in the future if they were asked to speak about their book. I have written my list of top-ten books for *Founding Fuel*.

C. I have got my share of criticism for one book—Rajat Gupta's *Mind Without Fear*. I don't know Rajat Gupta and have met him once at ISB (Indian School of Business) when I went to speak there. I summarized the book because it was his story of what happened. I was surprised to see negative comments from some CEOs, accusing me of colluding with the author to promote his book. I was really surprised that people write such stuff on social media without checking their facts.

D. I have received criticism, alternative points of view and negative comments on some of my posts. I accept them and try and tell the critic my point of view with a one-to-one message. If the person links anything I have posted to religion or politics, then I promptly block that person. I don't want to be part of such dialogue. I follow these rules to keep my audience free of angst they can do without.

The danger for a CEO is to delegate his social media handle or account. Getting your communications team or a junior to do this will never give the audience a feel of the real you, and you will not be able to connect well with them. I have seen this delegation go horribly wrong for a few companies and CEOs.

I manage my LinkedIn page myself. I read all the comments, and try to analyse what's working and what's not with every post. I do get valuable suggestions, which helps me do a better job with my next post.

Social media is here to stay. It is as risky or as safe as the boundaries you want to set and the content you want to share. I wish I had got on to social media prior to 2018!

In Conclusion

There is no doubt that the CEO role has become more complex and complicated at the same time.

BCG consultants Yves Morieux and Peter Tollman in their excellent book—*Six Simple Rules: How to Manage Complexity without Getting Complicated*—elaborate on what is happening to organizations. These are my takeaways from the book which impact the CEO dilemma:

1. Morieux and Tollman hypothesize that there is a complexity that has come in as a result of the number of things that a company has to report to its stakeholders today.

2. These requirements have become more numerous, are changing faster and, what's more, are often in conflict with one another.

3. BCG Institute for Organization has created a BCG Complexity Index. It shows that business complexity has multiplied six-fold since 1995. This metric works by tracking the evolution of the number of performance requirements at a representative sample of companies in the USA and Europe over a period of fifty-five years, from 1955 onwards, the first year the Fortune 500 list was released. In 1955, companies typically committed to between four and seven performance imperatives; today, they commit to between twenty-five and forty, that is, a six- to ten-fold increase in performance measures over this fifty-five-year period. (In the last decade, many more sustainability and diversity measures have been added, and I think more will get added this decade.)

4. Between 15 and 50 per cent of the measures that a company promises to track and report are contradictory to each other; in 1995, no measures were contradictory. Typical contradictory measures include: high-quality products at low prices, goods required to be innovative and produced efficiently, supply chains to be fast and reliable, service to be locally relevant and globally

consistent. When a company manages to break a paradox like this, it creates new sources of value.

5. The growth of complexity can be attributed to shifting trade barriers and ease of access to technology for the average consumer. This has brought about many more choices, whereby consumers are harder to please and will not accept compromises.

6. The number of stakeholders has multiplied. Companies must answer customers, shareholders and employees, as well as political, regulatory and compliance authorities. I feel that every man/woman with a network and a cause introduces a new measure for CEOs to think about. Each of these stakeholders has a specific demand and it's impossible for a corporation to satisfy one without hurting the other. When the IPL ran into rough weather on account of the betting scandal, a number of people and groups challenged PepsiCo and its sponsorship of the IPL, asking us to take a stance. PepsiCo ultimately walked away from the sponsorship. No one argued for the company to stay on, be it cricket fans or PepsiCo brand fans, simply no one. In today's social world, anyone can object to anything.

7. Business complexity is not the problem. This is an opportunity for companies that know how to leverage. The answer is to throw simplicity at complexity, and not throw complexity at complexity.

8. The real curse is not complexity but 'complicatedness', by which the authors mean the proliferation of cumbersome organizational mechanisms—structures, procedures, rules and roles that companies put in place to deal with

complexity. It is this internal complicatedness with its attendant bureaucracy that is destroying a company's ability to leverage complexity for competitive advantage. This internal bureaucracy stops an organization from getting anything done. A lot of the complicatedness is a result of outdated, ineffectual and irrelevant management thinking and practices. Having worked in MNCs all my life, I can sense that the average MNC has become a giant bureaucracy that has lost its appetite to grow and has also become a soft target in some country or the other, on some issue or the other. This has made the MNC a more culturally risk-averse organism, with everyone trying their best to maintain status quo as long as they can.

9. The BCG Institute for Organization created an index of the number of procedures, vertical layers, interface structure, coordination bodies, score cards and decision approvals over the past fifteen years. Across the sample size of companies, the index has grown 6.7 per cent annually, which, over a fifty-five-year period, yields a thirty-five-fold increase! I remember the budgeting process in one of the organizations I led. We would complete the budget and the capital expenditure (capex) approval took around 120 days after that. That means a third of the year was gone before we could get anything out of the capex proposed. I suggested to the HQ folks that maybe we could start the capex discussions four months prior to presenting the annual budget!

10. Managers and leaders in the top quartile of the most complicated organizations spend more than 40 per cent of their time writing reports and between 30 and 60 per cent

of their total work hours in coordination meetings, work on work. The BCG analysis shows that in complicated organizations, teams spend 40–80 per cent of their time wasting their time. It is not that they are idle; they are working harder and harder on non-value-adding work. Employees of such complicated organizations are three times more likely to be disengaged.

What Morieux and Tollman paint with the BCG research is the rule and not the exception; it is the norm. I have seen this at close quarters through the course of my career. Every CEO thinks he will buck this 'bureaucracy' trend. You can only do that if you are not scared of losing your job and your reputation.

If you are to have that level of confidence, you have to be an industry thought leader and have your own reputation, irrespective of the company you work for. That requires enormous hard work, voracious learning and a commitment to consistently doing the right thing.

Finally, I think it's important to recognize that being a CEO in India is uniquely challenging, given the complexity, diversity and ambiguity. But having been at that position for seventeen years, I can say that it is rewarding and gratifying in equal measure.

Postscript

The year of the pandemic, 2020, was unprecedented for society, for every company, for every family, and for every leader and professional.

In the last fortnight of December 2020, I spent time doing individual video calls with the families of about fifty colleagues at work. On these calls, I had the opportunity to speak with the colleagues' spouses, children and aged parents. The one word that describes how I feel about 2021 is *gratitude*. Incidentally, every family I spoke with echoed the same emotion.

On these calls, I also saw enormous confidence among young people; despite the pandemic, they were all optimistic about the future and their careers.

In 2020, we prioritized health, survival and family ahead of careers. The year tested both our confidence and resilience. It was a good year for reflection.

The year 2020 has brought fresh questions to the table: Do we work from home? Do we work from office? Will a hybrid model be the solution? In the past, the workplace props and culture changed from time to time; now, the concept of the physical workspace itself is challenged! The last word hasn't been said on this. Every company will devise new policies for 2021 and beyond.

The year has also brought other questions and dilemmas to the fore:

- Does one pivot and adapt or stay the course and re-focus?
- What constitutes good leadership?
- When should leaders be detail-oriented and when should they focus on the big picture?
- How marketable are my skills?
- How do I learn digital capabilities before it is too late?
- Should I stay in a company that has cut my salary or join a new company with a raise?

Being alert, proactive and agile has never been more relevant; organizations and individuals have had to rethink their strategy and adapt.

In the future, we will need leaders who move us to a horizontal collectivism mode, unlike the vertical collectivism mode that exists in organizations today. Good leaders will help connect people, functions, customers, ecosystem partners and companies to each other—they will facilitate and not dictate; they will listen more and speak less.

Leaders who have been in the information loop and decision loop on every detail through 2020 will now have to zoom out of the decision loop in many cases. That's difficult for a detail-oriented leader and easier for the big-picture leader.

The year 2020 has disrupted individual skills and capabilities. Every professional needs to get digitally fluent immediately, and every company needs to have a digital business model at the heart of their operations.

In the last nine months, I have talked at many webinars about work, disruption and career management. People are even more curious on managing a career now, as compared to before 2020.

There is no foolproof formula to succeed professionally; not everyone follows a linear career trajectory. There will be curve balls to face and dilemmas to navigate. The dilemmas discussed in this book will impact people differently— depending on their stage of life and their priorities, which evolve.

The past year has been disruptive for everyone. For anyone whose career is just beginning or someone thinking of switching careers, the future appears daunting. I hope that the perspectives and insights in this book will provide you with the confidence and clarity required to make the choices that give you success and happiness.

Thank you for reading the book, and I am more than happy to get your feedback on it.

Please write to shiv@shivshivakumar.com.

Acknowledgements

There are so many people to thank for the twenty-four-month journey of this book from idea to product. The people who saw merit in the idea were my ex-boss, Indra Nooyi, and the noted management thinker Ram Charan. Both spontaneously said, 'Good idea!'

Radhika Marwah, from Penguin Random House India, who has been there, nudging me to finish the book.

Nikhil Inamdar, journalist and author, who did all the interviews for the book. Sadiya Upade, who researched a lot of the data, put the tables together and helped with content.

Aarti Kelshikar, author of *How India Works*, who was both a sounding board and critical first editor of many chapters in the book.

Abhay Rajankar, for all his help on the cover design of this book.

Divya Karnal, who put the various edited versions into one final, printable version.

Thanks to Lakshmi, Vineet Gill, Vijesh Kumar, Shruti Katoch, Sumangla Sharma and Gunjan Ahlawat at Penguin Random House India, Karan Talreja, Sharmila Dutta, Ella Yadav, Ajendra Shaw and Manisha Singh at Autumn Grey, and Divya Karnal, independent brand digital professional.

All the people who generously gave their time to the book:

1. Anusha Shetty
2. Bhavya Misra
3. Chandramouli Venkatesan
4. Debjani Ghosh
5. Hari Menon
6. Harish Devarajan
7. Kirthiga Reddy
8. M. Damodaran
9. Meena Ganesh
10. Pavitra Singh
11. Piyush Pandey
12. Prakash Nedungadi
13. Priyanka Vijayakumar
14. Rakesh Kumar
15. Rama Bijapurkar
16. Rohit Kale
17. R.R. Nair
18. Ruchika Gupta
19. Sonny Iqbal
20. Sudhanshu Vats
21. Sujatha Duvvuri
22. Balaraman V.
23. Vani Gupta Dandia
24. Vivek Gambhir

Awards and Achievements

Shiv Shivakumar: Some Notable Recognitions

Distinguished Alumnus Award, IIM Calcutta, 2011
Distinguished Alumnus Award, IIT Madras, 2016
Best CEO, 2011
Best Brand Builder, 2009
Lifetime Contribution to Management, AIMA, 2014
Transformational leadership Award, Nokia, 2008
Horasis-KPMG Transformational India Leader, 2019
Asian Leader Award for Leadership, AAMO, 2020
Speak in Top Indian Speaker Award, 2019
Jury of ET 40 under 40, 2014–2018
Jury India Business Leadership Award, CNBC, 2014
Jury AIMA India Leadership Awards, 2013 onwards
Foods Innovation Award for Novel Teas, 1998
Unilever Global Beverages Innovation Award, 1998
Unilever Central Asia Middle East Innovation Award, 1999

Listed as one of the future leaders by *The Hindu BusinessLine*, 2000

Listed as one of the top five Indian marketers by the *Economic Times*, 2003

Asia Pacific Philips leadership award for turning the Philips's consumer electronics business profitable and competitive, 2005

Named 'The Brand Builder of the Year' by the Chief Marketing Officers' Council, 2008, and 'CEO of the Year', 2009

Shiv Shivakumar: Board Roles

Director, Philips India, 2004–06

Board of Governors, IIM Ahmedabad, 2012–17

Independent Director, Godrej Consumer Products, 2008–17

President, All India Management Association, 2012–13

Chairman, Mobile Marketing Association, 2014–19

Chairman, Advertising Standards Council of India, 2018–19

Advisory Board, Multiples Private Equity, 2013 onwards

Board of Governors, XLRI and XIMB, 2013 onwards

Board of Governors, IIM Udaipur, 2018 onwards

Non-Executive Chairman of Board, Burger King, 2019 onwards

List of Sources

Dilemma 1

1. https://www2.deloitte.com/global/en/pages/about-deloitte/articles/millennialsurvey.html
2. https://www.randstad.in/employer-brand-research/rebr-country-report-india-2019.pdf
3. https://www.livemint.com/money/personal-finance/indians-wealth-grew-5-2-in-2018-19-credit-suisse-report-11571660803961.html
4. https://indianexpress.com/article/business/employees-salary-hike-lowest-in-a-decade-aon-survey-6275506/
5. https://theprint.in/economy/indias-household-debt-has-risen-80-in-2017-18-it-could-bite-if-incomes-dont-grow/240695/

Dilemma 2

1. https://www.thehindubusinessline.com/on-campus/Planning-a-second-MBA-abroad-What-to-watch-out-for/article20709451.ece
2. https://www.assocham.org/newsdetail.php?id=5651
3. https://www.aicte-india.org/sites/default/files/India%20Skill%20Report-2019.pdf
4. https://economictimes.indiatimes.com/news/economy/indicators/india-slips-two-places-to-53rd-position-on-global-talent-ranking-switzerland-on-top/articleshow/66705009.cms?from=mdr
5. https://www.indiatoday.in/magazine/education/story/20191104-step-by-step-to-the-top-1612697-2019-10-26
6. https://theprint.in/india/education/21-fewer-indian-students-went-abroad-last-year-as-us-figures-see-biggest-drop/326433/
7. https://www.fortuneindia.com/enterprise/fewer-indians-applying-to-us-b-schools-gmac/102835
8. https://www.isb.edu/programmes
9. https://www.gmac.com/market-intelligence-and-research/research-insights/recruitment-and-marketing/return-on-investment-beyond-financial

Dilemma 3

1. https://theconversation.com/why-more-couples-are-choosing-to-live-apart-124532

2. https://www.thehindu.com/data/45.36-crore-Indians-are-internal-migrants/article16748716.ece

3. https://timesofindia.indiatimes.com/india/at-17-5-million-indian-diaspora-remains-largest-in-world/articleshow/71193046.cms

4. https://www.ey.com/Publication/vwLUAssets/ey-2018-relocating-partner-survey-final-report/$File/ey-2018-relocating-partner-survey-final-report.pdf

5. https://www.strategyanalytics.com/access-services/enterprise/mobile-workforce/market-data/report-detail/global-mobile-workforce-forecast-update-2017-2023

6. https://www.pwc.com/gx/en/managing-tomorrows-people/future-of-work/pdf/talent-mobility-2020.pdf

7. https://www.bcg.com/publications/2018/decoding-global-talent.aspx

Dilemma 4

1. https://www.gallup.com/workplace/231587/millennials-job-hopping-generation.aspx

2. https://www.randstad.in/employer-brand-research/rebr-country-report-india-2019.pdf

3. https://news.linkedin.com/2019/January/57--indian-professionals-would-consider-switching-careers-to-get#:~:text=The%20first%20Career%20Pathways%20India,they%20are%20increasingly%20keen%20on

4. https://content.randstadsourceright.com/hubfs/Global%20campaign/TTR/2019/report/Randstad-Sourceright-2019-Talent-Trends-Report-190118.pdf

5. https://www.randstad.in/employers/randstad-insights/hr-game-changers-2016.pdf

6. https://assets.kpmg/content/dam/kpmg/in/pdf/2018/04/KPMG-India-Annual-Compensation-Trends-Survey.pdf

7. https://www.thehindubusinessline.com/news/high-attrition-rate-continues-to-be-bane-for-companies/article24497691.ece

8. https://www.shrm.org/resourcesandtools/hr-topics/employee-relations/pages/toxic-workplace-culture-report.aspx

9. https://economictimes.indiatimes.com/jobs/people-analytics-is-future-of-hr-in-india-shows-linkedin-report/articleshow/73548647.cms?from=mdr#:~:text=The%2010th%20annual%20edition%20of,HR%20in%20the%20coming%20years.

10. https://hbr.org/2002/06/cultivating-ex-employees

11. https://qz.com/work/1444592/alumni-programs/

Dilemma 5

1. https://www.tsne.org/creative-disruption

2. https://uk.finance.yahoo.com/news/time-staff-got-fully-paid-sabbaticals-060054320.html

3. https://theswaddle.com/study-70-of-indias-working-women-fear-pay-cuts-on-resuming-work/

4. https://www.shrm.org/hr-today/trends-and-forecasting/research-and-surveys/pages/benefits19.aspx

5. https://www.forbes.com/sites/kateashford/2017/02/28/retirement-2/#58a446fc5033

6. https://www.cam.ac.uk/research/news/many-highly-engaged-employees-suffer-from-burnout
7. https://wiw-report.s3.amazonaws.com/Women_in_the_Workplace_2019.pdf
8. https://hbr.org/2017/08/research-shows-that-organizations-benefit-when-employees-take-sabbaticals

Dilemma 6

1. https://news.linkedin.com/2019/January/57--indian-professionals-would-consider-switching-careers-to-get#:~:text=The%20first%20Career%20Pathways%20India,they%20are%20increasingly%20keen%20on
2. https://www.mckinsey.com/featured-insights/future-of-work/jobs-lost-jobs-gained-what-the-future-of-work-will-mean-for-jobs-skills-and-wages
3. https://www2.deloitte.com/us/en/insights/focus/human-capital-trends/2019/talent-acquisition-trends-strategies.html
4. https://www.telegraph.co.uk/education-and-careers/0/midlife-career-switchers-professionals-starting/
5. https://blog.linkedin.com/2015/01/30/switching-industries-no-longer-means-starting-over
6. https://www.indeed.com/lead/career-change
7. https://business.linkedin.com/content/dam/business/talent-solutions/global/en_us/job-switchers/PDF/job-switchers-global-report-english.pdf
8. https://economictimes.indiatimes.com/markets/stocks/news/65-of-ceos-keen-to-switch-fields-survey/articleshow/63241982.cms?from=mdr

9. https://knowledge.wharton.upenn.edu/article/grass-is-not-greener-when-staying-put-in-a-job-pays-off/
10. https://www.aier.org/article/older-workers-happier-in-new-careers/

Dilemma 7

1. https://www.bcg.com/publications/2018/decoding-global-talent.aspx
2. https://www.mckinsey.com/~/media/McKinsey/Featured%20Insights/Employment%20and%20Growth/Global%20migrations%20impact%20and%20opportunity/MGI-People-on-the-Move-In-brief-December-2016.ashx
3. https://economictimes.indiatimes.com/nri/working-abroad/fewer-indians-willing-to-work-abroad-survey/articleshow/62371613.cms?from=mdr
4. https://www.cgdev.org/publication/does-development-reduce-migration-working-paper-359
5. http://bwpeople.businessworld.in/article/Decline-In-Indians-Looking-To-Work-Overseas-As-Trump-And-Brexit-Bite/17-10-2017-128874/
6. https://www2.deloitte.com/us/en/insights/focus/human-capital-trends/2019/alternative-workforce-gig-economy.html
7. https://assets.kpmg/content/dam/kpmg/xx/pdf/2019/10/2019-gapp-survey-report-web.pdf
8. https://www.forbes.com/sites/stuartanderson/2020/02/03/indians-immigrating-to-canada-at-an-astonishing-rate/#7772fa142b5f

9. https://economictimes.indiatimes.com/nri/visa-and-immigration/indian-its-h-1b-visa-woes-could-worsen-in-2020/articleshow/73077722.cms?from=mdr

10. https://www.economist.com/britain/2019/02/09/europeans-in-britain-are-packing-up-the-rest-of-the-world-is-moving-in

11. https://timesofindia.indiatimes.com/india/uae-is-top-gulf-workplace-for-indians/articleshow/67495783.cms#:~:text=Related%20Videos&text=MUMBAI%3A%20Emigration%20clearances%20granted%20to,in%202014%20at%207.76%20lakh.

12. https://www.bloombergquint.com/global-economics/as-india-becomes-wealthier-more-indians-leave-its-shores

13. https://www.expatexplorer.hsbc.com/survey/finding/218/young-professionals-who-move-early-succeed-even-earlier

14. https://www.randstad.in/employer-brand-research/rebr-country-report-india-2019.pdf

15. https://www.mckinsey.com/featured-insights/asia-pacific/asias-future-is-now

Dilemma 8

1. https://www.gemconsortium.org/economy-profiles/india

2. https://www.nasscom.in/knowledge-center/publications/indian-tech-start-ecosystem-leading-tech-20s

3. https://www.livemint.com/Companies/qOBduC3OBVpKTv9CpCYayH/Walmart-completes-16billion-buyout-of-Flipkart.html

4. https://www.bain.com/insights/india-venture-capital-report-2020/
5. https://www.economist.com/business/2020/03/12/indias-booming-startup-scene-is-showing-signs-of-trouble
6. https://www.ibm.com/downloads/cas/RG0W6AMB
7. https://www.orfonline.org/research/the-indian-startup-ecosystem-drivers-challenges-and-pillars-of-support-55387/
8. https://hbr.org/2018/02/research-what-happens-to-a-startup-when-venture-capitalists-replace-the-founder
9. https://qz.com/india/1159280/corruption-and-bureaucracy-will-be-the-biggest-challenge-for-indian-startups-in-2018/
10. https://www.livemint.com/companies/start-ups/as-india-s-unicorn-club-grows-investments-in-startups-will-increase-in-2020-11577881396950.html
11. https://www.randstad.in/employer-brand-research/rebr-country-report-india-2019.pdf
12. https://www.bain.com/contentassets/dd3604b612d84aa48a0b120f0b589532/report_powering_the_economy_with_her_-_women_entrepreneurship_in-india.pdf

Dilemma 9

1. https://hbr.org/2002/09/what-makes-great-boards-great
2. http://www.indianboards.com/pages/snapshot-reports.aspx?snap=AA
3. http://www.hunt-partners.com/displays/uploaded/File/TheIndiaBoardReport2015-16.pdf

4. https://economictimes.indiatimes.com/articleshow/66722540.cms?from=mdr&utm_source=contentofinterest&utm_medium=text&utm_campaign=cppst

5. https://economictimes.indiatimes.com/news/company/corporate-trends/more-independent-directors-take-the-exit-fearing-legal-scrutiny/articleshow/69883746.cms?from=mdr

6. https://www.outlookindia.com/newsscroll/independent-directors-lose-sheen-2000-quit-last-year/1581467

7. https://hbr.org/2019/09/research-when-women-are-on-boards-male-ceos-are-less-overconfident

8. http://www.primedatabasegroup.com/primegroup_logo/Women%20Directors%20In%20India.pdf

9. https://www.livemint.com/companies/news/more-women-are-joining-corporate-boards-but-very-few-get-the-corner-office-11583133282585.html